# Gardening

## from the Ground Up

# MAGGIE STUCKEY

*Illustrations by*
*Elizabeth Mason Thomas*

ST. MARTIN'S GRIFFIN
NEW YORK

# Gardening

---

ROCK-BOTTOM
BASICS FOR
ABSOLUTE BEGINNERS

---

## from the Ground Up

*Design by Songhee Kim*

ISBN 0-312-18101-9

First St. Martin's Griffin Edition: January 1998
10  9  8  7  6  5  4  3  2  1

*DEEPEST THANKS TO:*

*LIZ THOMAS,* FOR HER STUNNING TALENT AND SPLENDID
ATTITUDE.

*CAROLYN CLARK,* FOR RESEARCH ASSISTANCE AND GOOD
CHEER.

*BARBARA ASHMUN,* FOR THE LIST OF TOP 10 ROSES, AND FOR
FRIENDSHIP.

*MARY STEERMAN,* WHO GAVE ME A QUIET PLACE TO WORK
WHEN I SORELY NEEDED IT.

*HEATHER JACKSON,* AT ST. MARTIN'S PRESS, WHO IS WHAT ALL
EDITORS SHOULD BE.

# CONTENTS

"TIME SPENT WORKING IN YOUR GARDEN WILL NOT BE
DEDUCTED FROM YOUR LIFE."

—M.S.

his book is for absolute beginners—those folks who, if you handed them a tulip bulb, literally would not know which end was up. It is intended to be a quick and easy source of very, very basic information. The explanations are simplified, using plain, ordinary English to the greatest possible degree. My goal is to help you understand the why of things. Once you have the basic picture, you will find it easier to figure out what to do and how to do it.

## Using This Book

The main section of this book is organized into brief chapters arranged in alphabetical order. Some of the chapters describe a particular kind of plant—trees, shrubs, bulbs, etc. Others explain a concept of botany or walk you through the process of doing some gardening task. I imagine that you will skip around, turning to a specific chapter as you need to know about that particular topic.

> Before you start, take note of the fact that there is a glossary of common gardening terms in the back of the book. If you come across a word that's new to you, flip back to page 243; it's probably included. This is a bit of a nuisance, I know, but I hope it's less bothersome than being bored to death by reading endless repeats of the definition.

You will notice right away that many of the "plant" chapters include Top 10 lists. These are, I frankly admit, highly subjective. The lists do not represent any scientific or statistical research, just my own sense of some good, basic, reliable plants that will probably do well in your garden.

If you want a suggestion, one good way to begin is to read the chapter on Design; it will give you a grounding in the process of figuring out which plants to buy.

The other piece of information you need for this figuring-out process is this: What do the plants look like? To answer that question, you need to begin learning about individual plants, and the best way to do that in a hurry is to tap into other people's knowledge.

## Learning About Plants

Here are my suggestions for the best sources.

1. *Experienced gardeners.* The single best source of information is someone who lives near you and has been gardening for a while. Take my word for this: Any friends, neighbors, or family members who garden will be *thrilled* to show you their garden and answer your questions. Even total strangers will. If you don't personally know any experienced gardeners, walk around your neighborhood on a Saturday afternoon and strike up conversations with anyone who's out working in the garden. The nice thing about this, aside from meeting your neighbors, is that the chances are excellent you have just the same kind of soil they do, and they can tell you what works and what doesn't.

2. *Fellow members of your garden club.* I don't know of a better way to instantly surround yourself with knowledgeable gardeners. Visit several and find one you are compatible with.

3. *The information desk at your nearest County Extension Office.* Each state in the union has an agricultural college, with a statewide Cooperative Extension Service (jointly managed with the U.S. Department of Agriculture) and County Extension Offices throughout the state. The county offices are staffed with agricultural and horticultural specialists whose job it is to provide information to horticultural businesses and home gardeners in that specific region. Take the time to find the office in your county (look in the county government pages of the phone directory); the wealth of information they have will amaze you, and it's all free.

   Your question may be answered by a staff person or by a Master Gardener, specially trained volunteers who either know the answer or know where to find it.

4. *Master Gardeners.* Or you may decide to enroll in the classes and become a Master Gardener yourself. This concentrated program of education is offered in many states, sponsored by County Extension Offices with local experts as instructors.

5. *Classes.* If you keep your eyes open, you will find many class offerings on various gardening topics. Usually the instructors will be from your area and will know local conditions. Check out community colleges, adult education programs at public schools, parks departments, and other educational institu-

tions. Private consultants and teachers usually advertise their classes in local newspapers. Large nurseries and growers often offer classes about their plants, sometimes free.

6. *Local newspaper columnists or garden commentators.* Again, you'll be getting information about what works in your area.

7. *The staff at a large nursery or garden center.* You have to be a bit careful here. You want a place where the staffpeople *really* know what they're talking about; but when you find such a place, they're almost always busy. That's because they usually have a reputation for having quality merchandise as well as knowledgeable people, and everybody wants to shop there. If possible, visit at slow times, when the staff has more time to answer questions.

8. *Your favorite library or bookstore.* Don't overlook the obvious: books and magazines. Some of my favorites are listed in the back of this book.

9. *Mail-order catalogs.* They are some of the very best sources of information. Most catalogs use color photos and many of the catalogs are free—it's a fantastic way to learn what various plants look like. Of course you will realize that this is a commercial venture; the photos show the plants at their very best, and the descriptions can be, well, flowery. Still, they are a tremendous resource. In the Appendix of this book I have listed the catalogs that I particularly admire, both for their selection and for the clarity and accuracy of the information they provide.

10. *Botanical gardens and garden tours.* When all is said and done, there is no substitute for looking at the plants themselves. It is really the only way to learn how they look at various seasons and stages of growth, how large they get, the shape they assume when mature, and so forth. Learn where the public gardens are in your area, and visit them in every season. Same with botanical gardens; become a member, if possible—we all need to support them. Check your library or favorite bookstore for one of several guidebooks to gardens around the country, and schedule a visit to a garden on your next vacation.

Private gardens in your area may be open to the public on specific occasions, often in conjunction with a fund-raising event. Garden clubs also organize tours of local gardens.

As a new gardener, you have a wonderful adventure ahead of you, and many new digging-in-the-dirt buddies to meet, all of whom welcome you with genuine friendship. Gardeners are, you will soon find, the nicest people in the world—eager to help, to share their plants and their knowledge, to answer questions, and untangle mysteries.

Welcome, friend.

## ANNUALS

"*W*hat happened to my petunias? They were so pretty last year but they didn't come-back. What did I do wrong?"

You didn't do anything wrong. Petunias, and a lot of other wonderful garden plants, are in the group called *annuals*. That means they go through an entire life cycle—from seed to baby plant to blooming beauty and finally to seed again—in one growing season. They die at the end of the season, and nothing you can do will change that.

Many flowers and 99.9% of our vegetables are annuals. To fix the notion of "annual" in your mind forever, visualize the familiar garden vegetable known as a green bean; maybe you call it *string bean*. The seed that you plant in the ground is a bean. It germinates and grows into a plant, the plant makes flowers, the flowers fade away, and long bean pods develop where the flowers were. At this point you harvest the beans and eat them, effectively interrupting the natural process, but if you had left things alone, the individual beans inside the pods would become very plump. If they stayed on the plant until the pods shriveled and the mature beans dried, you'd have seeds again.

---

### Top 10 Annuals for a Sunny Garden

1. Marigold. Flowers in yellow to orange range.
2. Petunia. Many colors: white, pink-red-purple, yellow.
3. Cosmos. Pink, white, red.
4. Zinnia. Many colors.
5. Stock. Pink, purple, white, cream.
6. Lobelia. Blue, purple, white.
7. Salvia. Red, blue, pink, white.
8. China aster. Pink, purple, lavender, rose, white.
9. Poppy, Shirley, and Flanders. Comes in all colors except blue.
10. Snapdragon. Red, white, yellow, bi-colors.

---

Annual flowers are grown from seed too—if not by you, then by someone at a wholesale nursery. This is where new gardeners get confused: often we buy annual plants in starter packs at the garden center, and we never see the seed, so we may not realize that these are annuals. Yet the flower holds the reproductive elements that, once pollinated, will ultimately become seeds for next year. (The best garden centers help us out by grouping them together under big signs that shout "Annuals.")

An annual plant wants to do only one thing: make seeds. Every genetic impulse imprinted in its cells urges the plant to reproduce itself. Once it achieves that by setting seeds, it will stop producing flowers. And that is why when you grow vegetables, you should harvest the vegetables when they're young. Very mature vegetables send this message to the plant: "Okay, job done—here are your seeds," and vegetable production shuts down.

That is also the reason annual flowers put out so many flowers: they race to make seeds before the cold weather kills the plant. Keep the old flowers picked off; once they start turning to seed, the production of flowers will diminish.

---

### Tip: Annuals Forever

If you leave the flower heads on a few plants at the end of the season, and purposefully let them set seed, the seeds will fall to the ground and germinate next spring, weather permitting. This is known as *self-sowing* or *seeding down*. It doesn't always work (weather conditions and plant genetics play a role), but it's free so you might as well try it.

---

## Designing with Annuals

There are two basic ways to use annuals:

1. *As part of a combination planting, as filler adding bright splashes of color.* Annuals work very well in combination with perennials. Their longer bloom period will compensate for the visual gaps left when perennials are finished flowering. Low, compact annuals planted in front of taller perennials or perennials that carry their flowers high on the plant nicely fill in the space between the ground and the blossoms.
2. *Massed in one area by themselves or with other similar annuals.* An area devoted to a certain kind of plant is called a *bed,* and so annuals are sometimes referred to as *bedding plants.* The effect is either dramatic, if done well, or boring, if not. The mistake many people make is not using a large enough area; when all the plants are the same or similar, drama must come from scale.

# Growing Annuals

The wonderful thing about annual flowers is that they bloom for such a long period: all summer long and into fall, until frost. At the risk of boring you with the obvious, the downside is that, except for the reliable self-sowers, you have to replant them every year.

Gardeners fall into two camps when it comes to annuals: those who buy tray packs of small plants at the garden center, and those who prefer to start their own seeds. The arguments for seeds, and the techniques involved, are described in the Seeds chapter. Here we will concentrate on working with transplants—or *starts,* as they're sometimes called.

The advantages to using transplants are:

1. Someone else has already done the hard work of getting them off to a healthy start.

2. In effect, you get to "borrow" someone's greenhouse to get a jump on the season. The moment the weather is right, you can have plants ready to go with just one trip to the garden center.

3. If flowers are already showing, you can see for sure what color the flowers will be.

All things considered, most brand-new gardeners have better success with transplants: they're easier and they're faster.

### PLANTING

When you bring your pots and trays of annuals home from the nursery, if you can't plant them right away, set the plants outside in a shady, protected location. Check the moisture of the soil in the pots each day until you plant them. When you're ready to plant, follow the general directions described for containers in the Planting chapter.

Be especially careful about matted roots in annual packs and small pots; if inventory turnover at the garden center is slow, annuals can become rootbound faster than you'd believe. You must be very aggressive about tearing away this thick mat; if you don't, the plants will simply never take off.

Knowing exactly *when* to plant annuals is a tricky piece of timing. Unless you like seeing things die, you don't want to do it until after the last killing frost in the spring, whenever that is in your area (see Weather chapter). On the other hand, if you wait too long, the selection at the garden center is puny and you have missed a couple of weeks of growing time.

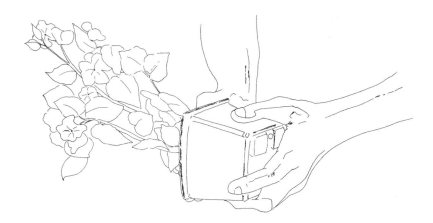

*Annuals often come in plastic pots. They may have been growing in them for a long time.*

*A dense snarl of roots echoing the shape of the bottom of the container (see page 7) must be cut away before planting.*

The trick is to find that window of time in between, when it is still coolish but it's not going to freeze anymore. Annuals planted during that "straddle" period will have time to establish a good root system before warmer weather triggers them to blast off. You may lose some early on (to a cold snap or slugs) and others will peter out toward the end of the summer. The great thing about annuals is, you just get some more and stick 'em in the ground.

### MAINTAINING

To keep your plants looking lush:

- Water often, especially during very hot weather. An inch of water once a week is optimal. Annuals tend to have shallow root systems, and can't tolerate a dry spell as well as other types of plants.
- Fertilize regularly with a complete fertilizer somewhat higher in phosphorus (see Fertilizer chapter). Because they have so much new growth, annuals are heavy feeders.
- Deadhead faithfully (pick off the dead flowers).
- Prune back if they get leggy (have long stems with flowers only at the outer ends).

## BIENNIALS

*Biennial* is the name for the group of plants that have a two-year life cycle. You probably won't have many of them in your garden, but you need to be aware so you won't be surprised by their unusual growth pattern.

In its first year, a biennial will produce only leaves. That first winter, the foliage will (usually) die back, but underground the roots are still alive. In spring of the second year, new leaves emerge from the ground. During the summer the foliage will grow much larger than it was the previous summer, and then the plant may produce flowers. Once it has flowered, the plant has fulfilled its genetic destiny (to reproduce itself), and when the weather turns cold, it will die completely.

But here's a nifty thing: in their second year many biennials drop their seed onto the ground, where they will germinate the following spring, starting another cycle. For a continuous supply, you need only to put in plants two years in a row; by the third year, seeds from the first year's plants will be sprouting.

Generally speaking, biennials are not spectacular in their first year. For that reason, often what you find in garden centers are second-year plants, ready to bloom. You should consider them self-sowing annuals.

ANNUALS

AND

BIENNIALS

## Top 10 Biennials

1. Forget-me-nots. Blue or pink flowers; self-sows (as do most biennials). Wouldn't be spring without them.
2. Foxglove. Tall, regal plant with cream, white, pink, or lavender flowers.
3. Canterbury bells. Blue, pink, white, purple.
4. Sweet william. White, pink, red.
5. Wallflower. Yellow, orange, burgundy, mahogany; often blooms in winter.
6. Feverfew. White, yellow daisylike flowers.
7. Hollyhock. Another tall plant, full color range (except blue).
8. Lunaria (money plant, silver dollar plant, honesty). Deep pink flowers; dried seed heads are this plant's highlight.
9. Peony-flowered poppy. Pink, red.
10. Echium (Vipers' bugloss). Blue, pink, and white flowers all on one stem.

## Annuals by Default

If a plant is not an annual or a biennial, it is a perennial, a plant which botanically speaking will live a number of years.

However, weather plays a role. So-called *tender perennials* will not live through cold winters, even though in every other respect they are perennials. As a practical matter, they are grown as annuals in colder regions, and sold as such by garden centers in those areas. Examples include coleus, dusty miller, gerbera daisy, geranium, verbena, primrose, rosemary, and, depending on the variety, some asters, salvias, spiderworts, spurges, begonias, and ferns.

T hey are often the first flowers we see in the spring, the clearest sign that the ice is breaking up and the waves of garden color are building. In fact, bulbs are so thoroughly identified with spring, you may not realize there are also summer-flowering and even fall-flowering types. There are bulbs whose flowers stand 4 feet high and more, and wee beauties that barely reach 4 inches.

## Types of Bulbs

Most people use the term *bulb* rather loosely, meaning any kind of fat underground storage system, but in truth there are five different types—true bulbs, corms, tubers, tuberous roots, and rhizomes (see illustration on page 12). They're treated pretty much the same, so for our purposes we can consider all these cousins to be bulbs.

## Designing with Bulbs

The foliage of bulb plants is essential for next year's flowers but it is not especially pretty: once it starts to die back, it is downright frumpy. Keeping this one botanical fact of life clearly in mind will help you visualize ways to include bulbs into your garden design.

- Plant spring-flowering bulbs tight up against summer perennials. The flowers of the bulbs will be in full glory while the first tiny shoots of the perennials are beginning to show; then the perennials, once full, will hide the yellowing foliage of the bulbs.
- Plant a low-growing evergreen ground cover right on top of bulbs. The bulbs will emerge up through the ground cover, which provides a dense, rich backdrop for the flowers and a disguise for the deteriorating foliage.

*(Left to right). A true bulb has layers of thick scales, like an onion. Examples: daffodil, tulip, hyacinth. Corms are squashed-looking and solid rather than layered; examples include gladiolus and crocus. Tubers, even flatter than corms, have roots all around the edges. Examples: anemones, caladiums, cyclamen, and tuberous begonias. Rhizomes look like very fat roots but are actually a type of underground stem. Examples: callas, bearded iris. Tuberous roots are fat, fleshy roots, easily separated into multiple plants. Dahlias and daylilies are examples.*

- Plant bulbs and herbaceous ground covers in the same spot. The bulbs will be up and blooming while the ground cover is just beginning to show signs of life; then the ground cover will fill in just when the bulbs are starting to peter out.
- Just as bulbs reach their peak of flowering, add small flowering annuals from six-packs right in among them. The growth rate of the annuals complements the fade rate of the bulbs, and by the time the bulb flowers are gone and foliage is ratty, the annuals are large enough to block it from view.
- Another botanical characteristic of many spring bulbs is their preference for dry soil in the summer, while they are manufacturing and storing food. That is one reason they do so nicely under deciduous trees: when fully leafed out, the branches keep the soil right around the trees dry.
- Bulbs work very well in mixed borders. Unlike perennials that get larger each season, bulb plants are the same size year after year. This makes them a valuable "building block" in borders designed in layers—that is, tiers of plants in varying heights.
- Small bulbs are wonderful additions to rock gardens, where their early color is a welcome pleasure.
- Whatever you do, plant *lots* of bulbs (rock gardens may be an exception). Individual tulips poking up here and there have nothing like the visual power of a mass of color.

- Who said bulbs always have to march in a straight line? Boring. Group them into several dense clusters, arranged by height, color, and bloom time, to create variety and seasonal rhythm.

---

### Bulbs: A Few Surprises

1. Peruvian daffodil (*Ismene*). Zones 8–10. Very exotic looking.
2. Crown imperial (*Fritillaria*). Zones 5–9. Very exotic, though not long-lived.
3. Voodoo lily (*Arum dracunculus*). Zones 8–10. Giant lily with spectacular purple/black blooms to 20 inches long, and a smell like rotten meat.
4. Belladonna lily, aka "Naked Lady." Zones 7–10. Foliage appears in spring, then dies back; in summer, on top of a bare stalk, suddenly beautiful large pink flowers appear, like amaryllis (a relative).
5. Erythronium. Zones 3–9. Wild lily with lovely spotted foliage and spring flowers.

---

## Bulbs for All Seasons

When you're designing a bulb planting and choosing the bulbs, remember that there are bulbs for three seasons: spring bloomers, summer bloomers, and fall bloomers. Some of the spring ones are so early we could even call them winter bloomers.

But even among the spring bulbs, there is a distinct sequence of timing.

*Early spring:* glory of the snow, crocus, snowdrop, bulb iris, winter aconite.
*Midspring:* Grecian windflower, siberian squill (scilla), daffodil, hyacinth.
*Late spring:* wood hyacinth, summer snowflake, star of bethlehem, hardy cyclamen, alliums.

Also, be aware that, even among the same species, different cultivars bloom at different times. There are, for example, early, midseason, and late tulips; there are early and late daffodils; and there are so many types of lilies that you can have lilies in bloom from spring through fall. Pay attention when ordering, and you can have flowers throughout most of three seasons.

# Planting and Caring for Your Bulbs

Bulbs are planted in the season before they bloom:

- Plant spring bulbs in the fall.
- Plant summer bulbs in the spring.
- Plant fall bulbs in the summer.

### PLANTING SPRING BULBS

Choose a site that gets full sun at least four hours a day. (Spring bulbs can tolerate partial shade after their bloom period is over, which is another reason they do well under deciduous trees.)

The soil must drain well, so the bulbs don't rot, with a pH between 6 and 7. If your soil is very heavy, take the time to work in some compost or other soil amendments (see Soil chapter). Also add in fertilizer at this point: bulbs especially need phosphorus and potassium to develop good flowers, and those nutrients work only when they are very close to a plant's roots.

There is a tool that makes planting individual bulbs easy, and it is called, amazingly enough, a bulb planter (see illustration on page 17). It is particularly handy if you are adding bulbs to an established flower bed. Insert the planter as far down as it will go, twist, and pull up a soil plug. Sprinkle in a bit of fertilizer, then place the bulb in the hole. Using your thumbs, push the soil plug out of the planter and back into the hole. Press it down lightly, and move on to the next one. (There is also a larger version, which you operate with your foot, not illustrated here.)

> ### Planting Tip
>
> Be sure to leave some kind of marker to remind you where bulbs are planted; you don't want to slice into a tulip bulb early next spring when you're digging a hole for something else.

Planting a large swath of bulbs is simpler if you dig out a large hole or trench rather than individual holes. Add fertilizer and place the bulbs one by one in the hole, then fill in with soil and cover with an organic mulch. Large bulbs should be spaced 4 to 6 inches apart, smaller ones 1 to 3 inches.

Many gardeners who have to contend with heavy clay soil and bulbs that rot in the excess moisture add a layer of pure sand to the bottom of the hole, put the bulbs right on top of it, then backfill as usual. Further, if you know burrowing rodents that eat bulbs can be a problem in your area, the time to take measures against them is before backfilling the hole. After you have loosened up the soil and added the fertilizer, but before you put in the bulbs, line the sides and bottom of the hole with wire mesh (such as chicken wire). The bulbs go on top of the wire, and then fill in all around with soil.

There is a relationship between size of bulb and size of plant and flower, and also between size of bulb and planting depth. Generally, the bigger the bulb, the

---

### Top 10 Spring Bulbs

1. Daffodil. Zones 2–9. Multiply themselves year after year, but slowly. In Deep South need to dig and chill bulbs, or grow them as annuals.
2. Grape hyacinth. Zones 2–9. Not a true hyacinth, multiplies easily by dropping its ripe seeds. Needs to be dug up and chilled in the South.
3. Tulip. Zones 2–9. Tulips are Mediterranean plants; they do best in soil that's on the dry side. They multiply slowly, and some varieties fade out after three to four years in some areas; need to chill if live in Deep South or grow as annual.
4. Crocus. Zones 3–8. Multiply rapidly; many varieties; among earliest bloomers.
5. Hyacinth. Zones 6–9. Need winter chill in South, or grow as annual.
6. Scilla (Spanish bluebells). Zones 4–9. Multiply rapidly.
7. Chinodoxa (glory of the snow). Zones 3–9. Multiply rapidly.
8. Ranunculus. Zones 8–10. Bulb increases in size each year; often grown as annual in cool climates.
9. Japanese anemone. Zones 8–10. Multiply moderately; often grown as annual in cool climates.
10. Snowdrop. Zones 3–9. Multiply rapidly. The very first bloomer on this list, sometimes as early as late winter.

---

### Planting Tip

Most of the time, it is quite obvious which end of a bulb is the bottom. But if ever you should be uncertain, lay the bulb on its side. The plant will figure it out.

---

deeper it goes. As a rule of thumb, the hole should be at least twice as deep as the diameter of your bulbs. The chart on page 17 shows the correct depth for some of the most popular bulbs.

## PLANTING SUMMER AND FALL BULBS

Imagine that you are planting annuals, and you'll know what to do. Choose a sunny location, give them lots of water and fertilizer (see below).

While the bulb flowers are blooming, you have no responsibilities except to love them (well, okay, water them if it doesn't rain at all and deadhead the faded flowers). But once the flowers fade, you have an important role to play.

When flowering is over, the plant goes into high gear, replenishing its nutrients. Bulbs, like all plants, manufacture their own food using chlorophyll in the foliage. What is unique about bulbous plants is that they then send that food down to the bulb for storage until next year. You can help this process in two ways:

1. Add a complete fertilizer right around the plant, in a ratio of 1/2/1; most so-called "bulb food" is something like 5/10/5, which is fine.
2. Resist the temptation to cut away the foliage, even if it looks ratty. Don't braid it, fold it over, or tie it with rubber bands; just leave it alone. Research at Cornell University has demonstrated that after six weeks, the bulb has produced enough food and sent it down underground. Leaving the foliage in place longer than six weeks won't significantly improve that, but don't remove it before that six-week period is over, no matter how tacky it looks.

---

### Top 10 Summer Bulbs

1. Dahlia. Zones 9–10. Dig and store in winter, zones 8 and colder. Multiply well; great range of colors and sizes.
2. Lilies: Asiatic, hybrid, tiger. Hardy zones 4–9. Multiply slowly; wonderfully fragrant.
3. Gladioli. Zones 9–10. Winter mulch needed in zone 8 or colder, or dig and store; multiply rapidly.
4. Canna. Zones 9–10. Dig and store in cold areas; bulb increases in size each year.
5. Alstroemeria. Zones 6–10. Multiply rapidly. Florist's favorite; fragrant.
6. Allium (ornamental onion). Many varieties, most zones. Unusual flower heads.
7. Cyclamen. Zones 5–9. Bulb increases in size each year. There are spring-, summer-and fall-blooming varieties.
8. Crocosmia. Zones 6–9; hardiness varies by variety. Gorgeous hot orange/red color.
9. Sparaxis (Harlequin flower). Zones 9–10. Grow as annual elsewhere. Delicate orchid-like flower.
10. Camassia lily. Zones 3–10. Blue, white, or yellow flowers in a cluster.

---

### THE SECOND YEAR, AND THEREAFTER

When it arrives in your life direct from a bulb farm or nursery, a bulb contains a complete plant (in embryo form). As long as it gets water and light, it will grow into a complete plant with roots, foliage, and flower . . . once. What it does the second year depends on the conditions it endured the first year.

Bulbs that bloom in the spring are called "hardy." That means that they will survive cold weather; in fact, they need it if they are to bloom the following spring. (In very warm climates, they should be dug up and stored in the refrigerator.) They also need the food-producing period after blooming, so they need

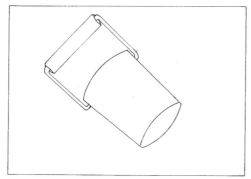

*A bulb planter makes it easy to dig holes just the right size.*

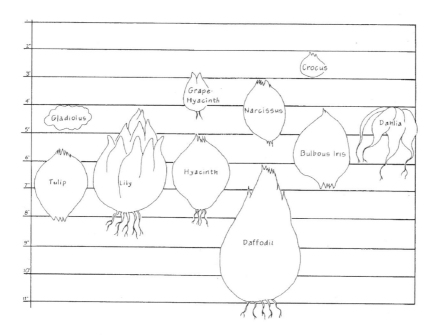

*Planting depths for some of the most popular bulbs.*

their guardians (that's you) to not mess with the foliage. They need soil that isn't so waterlogged they rot over the winter. And they need moles to leave them alone.

Life being what it is, they don't always get those conditions. Your hair can turn gray while you're waiting for the tulips from last year to bloom this year.

If you want a guarantee, plant new bulbs each year.

Most bulbs that bloom in summer and fall are called "tender," meaning they will not endure severe freezes. Unless you live in a mild climate, you will have to dig them up each fall and store them through the winter, and then replant next spring. The technique is not difficult; what's hard is remembering to do it.

As soon as the leaves turn black after a frost, dig up the bulbs, wash off the soil, and trim away the stem and foliage. Spread the bulbs in the sun for a few days, until they start to dry. Store them in a cool, dry spot (like the basement or garage) in a box filled with peat moss, sawdust, or vermiculite. Every now and then, push aside some of the peat moss. If the bulbs are starting to shrivel, dampen the moss; if they are sprouting, move them to a very dry spot until they dry out, then re-cover with dry moss.

An easier technique is to grow very tender bulbs in containers, and move the entire container into a protected place for the winter. Don't water or fertilize during this period.

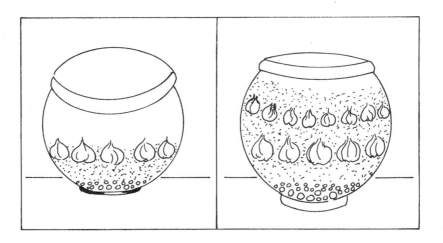

*For a spectacular and long-lasting display, plant two layers of bulbs in one container. Fill pot about one-third full with soil, add bulbs, then another layer of dirt and smaller bulbs. Top off with more soil and water well.*

*Gardening from the Ground Up*

## Bulbs in Containers

Bulbs grow very nicely in containers; if underground animals have been a problem in your area, this is a good way to keep them from digging up your bulbs. Plant just as you would in the ground, except place the bulbs very close together. You can also create a terrific effect by planting several layers of bulbs, with staggered bloom times.

Once the last of the bulb flowers are up, begin to fill in with trailing annuals. Use young plants that have small root systems, and be careful not to dig into the bulbs.

## Forcing Bulbs for Indoor Bloom

Remember that a first-year bulb contains everything it needs to produce a flower; soil is extraneous. When you are sick and tired of winter and yearning for a sweet breath of spring, this bit of botanical trivia will come in handy, for you can get

*Bulb containers can do double duty if you add small annuals as the bulb flowers are starting to fade.*

bulbs to bloom indoors earlier than they would outdoors. It is called "forcing" because we are forcing the calendar—manipulating the plant's environment so that it will bloom early.

In essence, the process involves giving bulbs a cold treatment (to simulate winter) and then water and light (to simulate spring).

---

### Best Bulbs for Forcing

1. Paperwhites—a type of narcissus.
2. Crocus—most varieties work well indoors.
3. Hyacinth—choose the large fragrant varieties.
4. Daffodils—miniatures are best.

---

1. Plant the bulbs in a pot with good potting soil; the tip of the bulbs should be peeking through the top.
2. Put the pot in a spot where it is dark and cool but not freezing: your refrigerator is perfect. The basement or garage is probably the right temperature; apartment dwellers can use an insulated picnic cooler on the balcony. Keep it in that spot until the bulbs have begun to sprout; depending on the plant, this could be two to three months. Don't water during this time, but don't let the soil or the bulbs become completely dried out either.

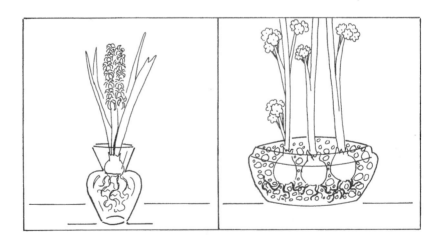

*Two common ways to force bulbs for indoor flowers early in the year: An old-fashioned hyacinth glass (left) holds the bulb steady and allows roots to grow down into water. Shallow bowl (right) holds paperwhite narcissi nestled firmly in among rocks and water.*

*Gardening from the Ground Up*

3. When shoots are about 2 inches tall, bring the pot into a warm and sunny spot.
4. If you plant several pots, stagger your schedule: bring them in to the warmth one at a time. That way, you'll have blooms for a longer period of time.

A variation on this process uses a container filled with pebbles, rather than potting soil; paperwhite narcissi are often done this way. The basic procedure is the same; keep the bulbs, nestled in among the pebbles, in a cold spot until they sprout. Then fill the container with water, and wait for the blossoms. Refill the water as it evaporates.

One thing you should be aware of: plants that are forced this way often develop abnormally long stems before they flower. Find some slender stakes, and keep them at the ready.

Another variation on this idea uses the classic hyacinth vase. This hourglass-shaped vase was designed just for forcing bulbs; it holds the bulb up above water, so that the roots grow down in but the bulb itself does not sit in water. The vases themselves have a wonderful Victorian look and feel, and a grouping of them in a sunny window is quite a sight.

In all cases, you will have much better success if you choose varieties that are especially recommended for forcing. Good mail-order catalogs often include their recommendations.

*I*t's probably too much to expect that your children will get excited about deadheading rhododendrons or pruning the hedge, but there is much in a garden to pique their interest. Then they're hooked, and the next generation of gardeners is assured.

To involve your children in gardening in a no-whine way, keep in mind some general guidelines, and be guided by common sense.

- Children have short attention spans; give them bite-sized tasks. And don't expect perfection.
- Children are fascinated by bugs and spiders; help them learn to tell the good guys from the bad guys. (See chapter on Problems.)
- Children are naturally attracted to small things of any species; just think how they go silly over puppies and brand-new kittens. For the same reasons, they enjoy watching plants grow from a seed to a baby plant to something recognizable.
- Learn which common garden plants have poisonous parts (see box on next page) and keep them away from children. Teach toddlers not to eat *anything* without a grownup at hand; teach older children to recognize toxic weeds and wild plants that may be growing in your area. Teach yourself, if you don't know; your County Extension office or local Poison Control center can help.
- Children feel more comfortable with things that are familiar; that's why they ask for the same bedtime story a jillion times. They will probably show more interest in carrots than camellias. Don't force the issue.
- Within reason, let children do things their way. When my niece was three, she liked watering "her" lettuce with a squirt gun. It didn't hurt the lettuce, and it helped her feel involved in the garden.

If you have the space, the very best thing you can do to foster children's interest is to give them a garden plot of their own. You will have to help prepare the bed and apply fertilizer; assistance with weeding is negotiable. But as much as practical, let them decide what to plant

---

### Poisonous Beauties

These are not necessarily the most dangerous of all toxic plants, but they are the ones you are most likely to have in the garden.

| plant name | toxic part if ingested |
| --- | --- |
| Autumn crocus | All parts |
| Daphne | Berries, bark, and leaves |
| Datura (angels trumpet) | All parts |
| Delphinium (larkspur) | Seeds, foliage, especially in young plants |
| Foxglove | Foliage, fresh or dried; seeds |
| Hydrangea | Leaves, flower buds |
| Lantana | Berries (may be lethal) |
| Poppy | Seeds, foliage |
| Narcissus, daffodil, jonquil | Bulbs |

---

and then do most of the care. I think you'll be surprised by their stick-to-itiveness.

Suggestions for kid-friendly plants:

- Sunflowers. They grow fast and children love hiding in a forest of the tall plants. For the adults, it's fun to watch the click of recognition when the children realize where sunflower seeds come from. Try to find the variety called 'Teddy Bear,' with short stems and big flowers.
- Potatoes. The children in my life find it fascinating to dig in the dirt and come up with a potato.
- Things that grow fast: radishes, lettuce, bush beans, zinnias, sunflowers.
- Pansies, because they look like cat faces.
- Cherry tomatoes or those wonderful small yellow pear tomatoes. They are one-bite treats you can eat as is, and the fruit is right at their eye level. I've never met a child who didn't like picking them and eating them right in the garden.
- Fennel. They probably aren't interested in herbs the way you are, but children are amazed that the frilly foliage of this plant tastes like licorice.

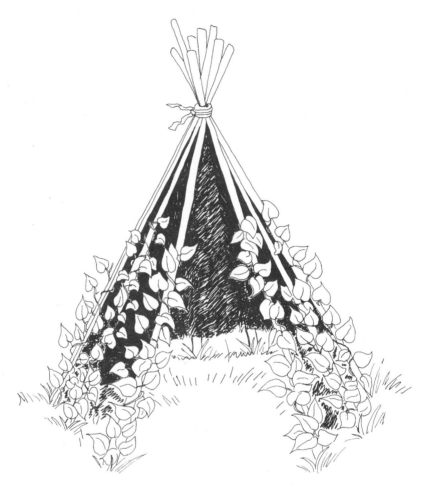

*What little kid could resist hiding in this tepee made of pole beans?*

## Gardening Projects for Children

Here are some specific ideas with built-in "kid appeal."

- *Make a tepee of beans.* Set several long poles or pruned tree limbs in a circle, leaving a gap for a doorway. Lash the tops together, and plant pole bean seeds at the base of each pole (five or six per pole). Of course this works with any vining plant, but with beans you get a bonus: something good to eat.

- *Grow autographed pumpkins.* When young pumpkins are about the size of a canteloupe, let children carve their name in the skin (the pumpkin stays attached to the plant). Easiest way is to write the name with a felt tip pen and go over it with a nail or knitting needle; very young children may need help. Then leave the pumpkin to grow as usual. The carving will scar over, and the mature pumpkin will be personalized.
- *Plant a small vegetable garden of their favorites.* Whatever they like goes in, whatever they hate stays out.
- *Grow flowers for bouquets.* Concentrate on varieties that grow fast and are relatively trouble-free: cosmos, zinnias, marigolds, or bachelor's buttons, for example. The idea here is to tap into the same feeling that makes children assemble a bouquet of dandelions for Grandma, but provide them better plants to do it with. Let them pick the flowers and give them to whomever they choose. Older children might like to set up a sidewalk stand and sell their flowers.

*I*t is easy to be seduced by the brash "look-at-me" colors of flowers and overlook the subtler but no less beautiful color contributions of leaves, bark, and berries. In well-designed gardens, color comes from all these sources in harmonious, artful blendings. With careful planning, you can have color year-round.

## Color from Flowers

Flowers, of course, are the most obvious way for you to get color into the garden. The range of possibilities may seem overwhelming at first—there are so many flowering plants in so many shades of color. By browsing through garden magazines and books featuring color photos, and visiting gardens whenever you can, you'll gradually build up your own list of favorites.

Perhaps the most helpful thing I can do is give you some general guidelines. First, some rules of thumb about color intensity.

- Most annuals and bulbs have strong, vivid colors.
- Perennials tend toward the softer shades.
- Flowering trees are primarily pastels.
- Most flowering shrubs have deeply saturated color.

Another consideration is how long the flowers last. While there are all kinds of exceptions, speaking very generally we can say that:

- Annuals stay in bloom longest—from early summer up till frost.
- Perennials bloom for a month or more, especially if you keep deadheading them; if you cut them back after flowering sometimes they will put on a second bloom late in the season.

- Flowering shrubs and trees have a shorter blooming period, measured in weeks rather than months.
- Bulbs are a brief, bright flash of intense color.

Finally, let us consider the question of flowers from a seasonal perspective. Remember, the lists here are simply to get you started. They do not pretend to be complete and they do not allow for the thousands of exceptions.

### WINTER FLOWERS
Winter-flowering varieties of ornamental cherry trees
A few shrubs (camellia, sweet box)
A few perennials (hellebores)
Very early bulbs (snowdrops, crocus)

### SPRING FLOWERS
Bulbs
Most flowering trees (cherry, plum, pear, crabapple, hawthorne, dogwood, tulip tree)
Shrubs (forsythia, lilac, azalea, rhododendron, viburnum)
Some perennials (peony, bleeding heart, poppy, phlox)

### SUMMER FLOWERS
Some flowering trees (crepe myrtle, magnolia)
Annuals
Most perennials
Roses
Summer bulbs (dahlia, gladiola, lily)
Vines (clematis, honeysuckle, passion flower)

### FALL FLOWERS
Some perennials (aster, daisy, chrysanthemum, anenome, hydrangea, certain sedums)
Many annuals carry into autumn

## Color from Foliage

When someone talks about colorful leaves, we usually think in terms of autumn color. And a magnificent color display it is, definitely worth planning for. (See list on page 31.)

Here, though, I wish to introduce you to the idea that some plants have colored leaves all the time.

Foliage color can take several forms:

- Leaves are a distinctly different shade of green: a bright chartreuse that is more yellow than green, or a rich blue-green.
- Leaves are some color other than green: magenta, purple, burgundy.
- Leaves are a mixture of colors, what we call variegated.

Variegated foliage means that each leaf on the plant contains at least two colors, green and something else. The second color may be white, cream, pink, chartreuse, yellow, burgundy, etc. It may appear on the leaf as dots, stripes, or circles, a border around the edge of the leaf, or irregular blotches. Plants with variegated foliage in three colors are less common but quite spectacular.

---

### Shrubs with Colored or Variegated Foliage

1. Euonymous. Several varieties; low shrub to small tree. Most are hardy zones 5–9. Some foliage is green and silver/white, some has bright yellow edge. Leaves can be large or small. Evergreen in mild climates.
2. Aucuba. Zones 7–10. Rich green leaves dotted with yellow. Several varieties, 5 to 8 feet. Evergreen in mild climates.
3. Weigela. Zones 4–9. Deciduous flowering shrub in several varieties. One has burgundy red foliage with wine-colored flowers; another has cream/green variegated foliage and pink flowers. Grows to 8 feet.
4. Leucothoe. Zones 5–9. Tricolor foliage in red/cream/green. Evergreen in mild climates. Grows to 5 feet.
5. Pieris (Japanese andromeda). Zones 7–9. Cream/dark green leaves; new foliage is red. Has small white winter flowers. Evergreen in mild climates. Grows to 10 feet.
6. Golden hinoki cypress. Zones 4–8. Dark green needles with yellow tips. Evergreen. Grows to 20 feet; a miniature type grows to four feet.

---

## Trees with Colored or Variegated Foliage

1. Tricolor dogwood. Foliage is white/pink/green, flowers are pink or white. Deciduous; grows to 20 feet; blooms in spring.
2. Variegated turkey oak. Zones 7–9. Glossy, dark green leaves, edged in creamy white. Deciduous tree, grows to 50 feet in height.
3. Variegated box elder. Zones 3–9. Bright green leaves edged in pink turning to white. Deciduous and grows to 50 feet.
4. Sunburst honey locust. Zones 5–9. Sunny yellow foliage. Deciduous, to 50 feet.
5. 'Crimson King' red-leaf maple. Zones 4–7. Deciduous, to 100 feet.
6. 'Royalty' crabapple. Zones 5–8. Crimson foliage. Deciduous, to 30 feet.
7. Colorado blue spruce. Zones 3–8. Bluish needles. Evergreen, to 50 feet.

## Ground Covers (and a Few Perennials) with Variegated Foliage

1. St. Johns wort (*Hypericum*). Most types hardy to zones 7–9. Green/yellow/red variegated leaves. Grows 6 inches to 3 feet.
2. Variegated periwinkle (*Vinca variegata*). Zones 7–9. Green leaves with cream-colored edge. Grows 6 to 12 inches.
3. Variegated juniper. Zones 5–9. Foliage is blue-green with cream-colored tips. Grows to 30 inches.
4. Carpet bugle (*Ajuga*). Zones 3–8. One variety has pink/white/purple variegated foliage. Grows 4 to 18 inches.
5. Epimedium. Zones 5–9. Light green, heart-shaped leaves with pink edge. Grows 12 to 18 inches.
6. Snow-in-summer. Zones 3–8. Forms a silver-white mat with white flowers. Grows to 6 inches.
7. Variegated ivy. Numerous varieties for nearly all zones. Green leaves splotched with white, cream, or yellow.
8. Houttuynia. Zones 5–9. Crazy mix of pink, green, yellow, and a marbly white. Grows 12 to 18 inches and spreads rapidly.
9. Euonymous. Zones 5–9. Green foliage with silver or yellow markings. Low-growing varieties stay 1 to 3 feet.
10. Variegated thyme. Zones 5–9. Several varieties, cream or yellow edging on leaves. Generally grows 6 to 12 inches. Lemon thyme is especially pretty.

## Color from Bark

Most people never give bark a second thought, until they come face to face with something extraordinary. In the city where I live, there is a ribbon-bark cherry tree in our magnificent Japanese garden, and I love to watch visitors react to it. The tree trunk looks for all the world like spools of wide ribbon stacked on top of one another, which is where the name comes from. The bark is the color of copper and has both the texture and the glow of satin. The color is so rich, and the surface so smooth, that no one can pass by without rubbing it.

Trees with colorful bark make their contribution to the garden year-round, becoming even more noticeable in winter, when their leaves are gone. A special winter position of honor goes to deciduous shrubs with colored limbs. The bright red stems of red-twig dogwood poking up through snow-covered ground, for instance, are quite a sight.

---

### Trees with Colored Bark

1. Eucalyptus. Zone 8 and warmer. Evergreen with multicolor peeling bark. There are many varieties, with quite different leaf shapes and distinctive fragrance; size varies from 30 to 150 feet.
2. Stewartia. Zones 7–9. Deciduous; peeling bark is tan and several shades of green. Grows to 50 feet.
3. Madrone. Zones 7–9. Evergreen with orange peeling bark. Grows to 50 feet.
4. Coral bark maple. Zones 6–8. Deciduous with light orange bark. Grows to 30 feet.
5. Cork oak. Zones 7–9. Evergreen with tan cork bark. We get our cork from the bark of this tree. Grows to 60 feet.
6. Paper (white bark) birch. Zones 2–8. Deciduous with white splotched bark (this is the famous "canoe birch"). Grows to 60 feet.

---

## Color from Berries

Berries are found on both deciduous and evergreen plants. They usually make their appearance in the fall and winter, at a time when the more obvious strata of color have disappeared from the garden. They give us a range of possible colors: white, red, orange, pink, purple, blue. They are either loud or subtle, competely covering the plant or hiding beneath the foliage. And a wonderful bonus for city-folk: They attract birds to your garden.

## Trees and Shrubs with Colored Berries

1. Hawthorn (tree); red or orange berries, in fall.
2. Madrone (tree); red/orange berries, late summer.
3. Mountain ash (tree); red, orange, or yellow berries, late summer.
4. Holly (tree); red or yellow berries, winter.
5. Persimmon (tree); familiar orange fruit on trees in winter.
6. Callicarpa (beautyberry) (shrub); lavender berries in fall through winter.
7. Barberry (shrub); red, orange, blue, yellow berries, depending on variety, in fall to winter.
8. Snowberry (*Symphoricarpos alba*) (shrub); white berries, fall/winter.
9. Pernettya (shrub); pink or white berries, fall/winter.
10. Clerodendrum (tree); berries are blue with pink base, leaves smell like peanut butter, fall/winter.

## Top 10 Trees for Fall Color

1. Sweet gum. Leaves are a mix of red, orange, and yellow.
2. Sumac. Intense red.
3. Aspen. Incandescent yellow.
4. Pin oak. Brilliant red.
5. Sourwood. Red with tinges of yellow and green.
6. Vine maple. Yellow/orange/red.
7. Sassafras. Red.
8. Dogwood. Red.
9. Japanese parasol tree. Bright yellow.
10. Tricolor beech. Burgundy red/pink/cream.

**COMPOST**

*S*avvy gardeners call it "black gold"—that gorgeous, rich, dark, fluffy stuff that comes out of the bottom of the compost pile. You can just tell by looking at it that plants will go wild for it.

Compost is the end product of the decomposition of organic material such as leaves, grass clippings, tree trimmings, and kitchen and garden debris. When we see a pile of decayed plant material, we might think that it just happened—these leaves just rotted on their own. But, in fact, they had help.

The decomposition process is the handiwork of microorganisms that live in soil—bacteria, fungi, and an assortment of worms. These microorganisms, most so small we cannot see them, use organic matter as food. They work away at the leaves, pine needles, and whatever else falls on the soil they inhabit, breaking it down into smaller and smaller pieces and leaving behind their own waste products.

*Composting* is the deliberate act of creating conditions where that decay is encouraged in large quantities; *compost* is the end result.

It is possible to purchase bagged compost in garden centers. For container gardening or preparing a spot in the garden for just one or two plants, this is a sensible way to go. But for any larger quantity of compost, I suspect you'll eventually want to make your own. It's practically free and it's extremely satisfying—a very righteous thing to do with all your yard debris and kitchen scraps.

There are two basic ways to go: a simple pile, or some kind of container, usually called (no matter what shape it is) a bin.

*Compost Piles*

Here's the easiest way to make compost: collect all the vegetative organic material you can get your hands on and pile it into something like a flat haystack. Let the rain and snow fall on it; water it now and then during dry spells. After about a year, pull away whatever is still in large pieces—tree branches, for instance. Underneath will be a bed of yummy compost. It is the texture of soil but extra-rich and dark in color.

The problem with this method is that it takes a long time. In addition to the plant parts that are their food, soil microorganisms need both air and water to live. You can depend on the weather to provide water and the gradual sifting and shifting of branches and leaves to provide the air, but if you take an active role, you can speed up the process. Do one or all of the following for compost in a flash:

- Lightly till the soil underneath the pile before you start laying on materials, to make it easier for worms to climb through and into the debris.
- Chop up all the material into small pieces before adding to the pile.
- Water the pile lightly about once a week if it doesn't rain.
- Alternate layers of soil (with their armies of microorganisms) with layers of debris.
- Introduce air into the center of the pile, via one of these techniques:
  Stick a garden fork down in several spots and wiggle it around.
  Turn the pile over; put the bottom on the top or the left half on the right side.
  Take a length of fat plastic pipe, drill holes all around it, and stand it upright in the pile.

## Compost Bins

For both esthetic and practical reasons, many composters prefer to use some kind of container instead of a free-standing pile. Compost bins make it easier to turn the material, allow you to move material in stages as it decomposes, and prevent the material from sliding away. They also present a tidier appearance.

A bin can be constructed from simple materials such as chicken wire or lumber, or a plastic garbage can with the bottom cut away and holes drilled in the sides. Remember that air needs to get into the pile. Alternatively, you can purchase a ready-made bin in any of a dozen shapes and materials.

Fully enclosed bins, either commercial or homemade, protect the composting material from weather and discourage neighborhood animals from poking in. The more artful the bins, the easier it is to forget they are there. You will have to figure out some system to remind yourself to turn and water the contents. Put it on

*Compost bins can easily be made from circles of heavy wire grid (left) or wood frames with wire ends. The square bin on the right was made with a removable front, to make it easier to turn the compost layers.*

your calendar at two-week intervals until you develop the habit, or mentally connect it to something else that you do on a regular basis.

A compost pile that is actively working is hot—and that's good. If you can maintain high temperatures (between 120° and 150°), you can produce workable compost in just a few weeks, as opposed to months. The way to keep the pile hot is to turn it very often, a tedious procedure if done by hand. A much easier system uses a tumbler bin—some kind of drum mounted horizontally, with a crank. This is extremely easy to turn, and because it also heats up fast, compost can be produced in as little as two weeks.

## What to Put in a Compost Pile

Leaves from the autumn raking
Grass clippings (dried)
Trimmings from garden plants and houseplants (as long as they are not diseased)
Weeds (no seed heads, though)
Old potting soil
Kitchen vegetable and fruit scraps

Crushed eggshells
Tea bags
Coffee grounds (along with filters)
Paper and newspaper (shredded first)

DON'T INCLUDE:
Meat or fish scraps from the kitchen
Cheese or dairy products
Pet waste
Coated paper (like magazines)

*G*rowing your garden in containers is a necessity if you don't have a yard, and a great convenience even if you do. With containers you can:

- Move your garden into and out of the sun.
- Fill in bare spots in flower beds.
- Plant a garden on top of hard surfaces like walkways and steps.
- Move the garden into a protected area in harsh weather.
- Rejuggle color combinations without digging anything up.
- Experiment with new plants without committing precious garden space.
- Bring the garden indoors in winter.

Every garden, no matter its size, site, or composition, is enhanced with container plantings. And there is virtually no limit to what you can grow in containers:

- Flowers and combinations of flowers (both annuals and perennials)
- Bulbs
- Roses
- Shrubs
- Small trees
- Vegetables
- Herbs

Houseplants are, of course, container plants too, but they are generally thought of as their own separate category, so in this book they have their own chapter.

> ### The First Law of Containers:
> They need to be watered faithfully.

# Designing the Container

When thinking about what to put in your container, remember that it is essentially a garden plot in miniature, portable form. The same principles of design apply. You need to think about proportion, balance, texture, and a harmonious blending of colors.

If anything, you need to be even more aware of good design in container gardens because containers will be viewed from close up. Mistakes will be more obvious, and there will be no overall background to soften and camouflage jarring colors or frumpy foliage.

Let us consider the many types of plantings from a design standpoint.

### BULBS

Bulbs do very nicely in containers. For the best display, plant the bulbs very thickly. Two general approaches to designing a bulb container garden are:

*Containers need lots of water. The hose at left is fitted with a "bubbler," which disperses the flow and prevents the stream of water from gouging a hole in the soil. Make provisions for reaching hanging containers, such as adding a spray nozzle to your hose.*

- Plant several types of bulbs together in the same container at different depths. This will give you a longer period of flowering. (See Bulb chapter.)
- Plant a combination container: bulbs for early spring, topped with seeds of summer annuals. As the flowers fade and the foliage starts to look ratty, the annuals will be taking hold. Variation, to get faster results: add small annual plants as soon as they show up in the market.

### ROSES

Miniature and patio roses seem made to order for containers. (See chapter on Roses.) There's no real design finesse needed here; the rose will want to be in the container by itself.

### SHRUBS

Small evergreen shrubs in matching containers look nice framing a doorway, especially if they are enhanced with a small trailing plant that droops over the edge of the container, providing balance to the upright lines.

Flowering shrubs provide a strong splash of color along with the foliage. For visual proportion, select a small or even a dwarf variety.

---

**Small Trees That Do Well in Containers**

1. Japanese maples. There are several small varieties, all deciduous with wonderful fall color.
2. Crepe myrtle. Deciduous. Beautiful flowers in late summer, good fall foliage color.
3. There are several varieties of small evergreen trees: alpine firs or pines and/or Alberta spruce.
4. Figs. Deciduous. There are both fruiting and ornamental varieties. Bring inside in winter.

---

### TREES

You will of course need a large container and a small tree. But within those parameters you can grow trees in containers. (If you don't believe me, think of that weeping fig in the lobby of your bank.) Here again, you may want to plant trailing or vining plants underneath the tree to soften the edges and give visual balance.

### VEGETABLES

If you have enough sun, and can be faithful about watering, you can grow many kinds of vegetables in containers. Concentrate on plants that don't take up much space (lettuce, scallions, chard) or that can be staked to grow upright to maximize

*Containers planted with a blend of many types of flowers, or flowers together with herbs, offer concentrated color.*

space (patio tomatoes, peppers). Above all, choose varieties of your favorite vegetables that stay small and compact. Many seed catalogs suggest varieties that are especially appropriate for containers. (See Vegetable chapter for more suggestions.)

### HERBS

Herbs are a natural for growing in containers, for lots of reasons:

- Most herb plants are small and tidy, and thus fit well in containers.
- Something about them entices people to lean close and fondle them, and this is much easier to do when they're in close-by containers.
- You want them close at hand for cooking, just by the kitchen door, or on the windowsill.
- Herbs lining the walk and stairs to your front door make a welcoming entrance. Not only are they pretty to look at, but brushing against them releases a wonderful fragrance.

You will probably want to stay away from the plants that get really huge (angelica or dill, for example), but other than that you can grow in a container any herb you can grow in the ground. Here are a few suggestions; the first three are combination plantings:

- Basil, cinnamon thyme, and tarragon.
- Variegated sage and lemon thyme.
- Parsley, chives, and oregano.
- Any kind of mint; mint actually does better in containers than in the ground, where it spreads madly and takes over everything.
- Lavender—put it by the front walkway.

## FLOWERS

Far and away the most popular plants for containers are flowers, probably because they make the biggest impact. And if your only garden is a container or two, you want all the punch you can get.

You can use all annuals or combinations of annuals and perennials. Combining flowering plants with plants that have colorful foliage is very appealing.

There are so many possibilities for flower containers, it is downright foolish for me to list specific plants. Instead, I offer some general guidelines (see box) and suggest that you browse the photos in some of the many good books about container gardening.

For good color combinations, wait till blooming annuals start to show up at the garden centers. Shop for all your container plants at the same nursery on the same day. As you add plants to your shopping cart, study how they look together: compatible colors, good texture contrast, and so on.

---

### Flower Container Guidelines

- Plant together, in the same container, plants that have the same needs for water and for sunshine. If you mix them up, you'll never be able to find a happy medium for everything you've planted.
- If you do a mixed container, with several different plants, view the container as a miniature landscape. Put something tall in the center, something trailing near the edge, and mid-size plants in between.
- Containers are very concentrated visually, so be very careful with color combinations. Colors that clash are especially disconcerting when they are so very close together.
- Plan things that bloom at the same time, to show off the color blends.
- To really make an impact, use larger pots—18 inches or more. Or cluster several smaller ones together. Make the grouping more interesting by using containers of varying heights. For a tall look, turn one empty pot upside down and use it as a pedestal.
- When planting annuals, start with good-size transplants and put in lots of them. As the season progresses, replace them when they look bedraggled.

---

# Types of Containers

**Clay** is the classic material for pots large or small. It is porous and lets air through into the soil, which is a good thing. For the same reason it tends to dry out more rapidly than other materials. In large sizes, it is quite heavy. If left outside in very cold weather, clay pots often crack when water in the pores freezes.

**Plastic** is probably the most economical material for containers. Another advantage: it holds moisture in longer.

**Wood** is attractive but direct contact with moist soil will eventually decay it.

**Ceramic, brass, and other decorative materials** should be considered display pieces, unless you have more money than you know what to do with. Use them as outer containers, with a pedestrian plastic container inside.

**Wood pulp** looks like cardboard with a pebbly texture, and that's essentially what it is. These containers are nice and lightweight, but will not last more than a couple of seasons.

All of these containers come in a very wide range of sizes. The smaller ones work well for houseplants, but for outdoor container gardening, use at least a 12-inch pot. (Pots are measured by their diameter at the top.) Anything smaller than that will dry out so quickly you simply will not be able to keep up with the watering.

---

**The First Law of Pots:**

They must have drainage holes. No exceptions, no arguments. If you have splurged on a beautiful brass urn and don't want to drill a hole in it, the only way you can plant in it is to use an inner pot that does have a drainage hole.

---

# Getting Ready to Plant

## SOIL

The same soilless potting mix you would use for houseplants also works for outdoor containers (see Houseplants chapter). But those mixes tend to dry out faster than a soil-based mix, a problem that is exacerbated outdoors. If you have several large containers (and adequate work and storage space), it may work out better to purchase large bags of these individual components and mix your own.

- Sand. You want builder's sand, not sand from the beach (the salt is harmful to plants).
- Peat moss.
- Topsoil or garden loam.

A blend in equal proportions will give you a good all-purpose potting mix. If you're going to grow acid-loving plants, use a double quantity of peat moss.

You can, if you wish, substitute either vermiculite or perlite for half the sand (read about them in Houseplants); this will give you a mix that weighs less, a real consideration in very large containers.

Cover your work space with newspapers or an old shower curtain; this is a wet, messy procedure. Rather than trying to mix right in the individual planting containers, use an extra large bin or bucket for mixing; a wheelbarrow works well, if you have one.

### SOIL POLYMERS

You're going to hear this from me several times: the biggest problem with outdoor containers is keeping them from drying out, especially in the dead of summer. One way to give yourself a little insurance is with a relatively new product known as soil polymers.

These are little pellets of a very lightweight material that is highly absorbent; they soak up water, hold it in a gel-like concentration, and slowly release moisture into the surrounding soil as they dry out. When dry, the granules look something like rock salt; they absorb many times their own weight in water, swelling in size several-fold. When thoroughly wet they look like globs of clear Jell-O. The granules themselves are extremely lightweight, so you are not increasing weight when you work them into the soil.

This product is not inexpensive, but you don't need much per container— about 1 tablespoon of the granules per 3-gallon pot. And the polymers last several seasons.

### FERTILIZER BEADS

Another item to work into the soil before you start planting is a measure of time-release fertilizer granules (see page 62). Because the frequent watering leaches away fertilizer, you're going to need to fertilize containers more often than you would an in-the-ground garden, and these fertilizer beads will shorten your task.

# Planting Your Container

In your big mixing bucket, combine all the components—soil mix, water-holding polymers, and fertilizer granules. Dampen everything well and mix again thoroughly.

If you are working with a very large container, say two or three feet in diameter, it will probably be as deep as it is wide. If you fill that whole thing with potting mix, it's going to be quite heavy. Unless you're planting a tree or shrub, you don't need the full depth of soil.

Make things easier on your back by filling the pot partway with either empty soda pop cans or foam peanuts, making up somewhere between one-third and one-half the height.

Some people object to the foam peanuts because if you ever decide to discontinue a container and want to dump its soil out into the garden, you have all those flyaway peanuts to retrieve. (That's one reason I like using soda cans.) But if you keep it as a container garden year after year, you don't have that problem.

**Planting a shrub, a tree, or a rose** in a container is quite similar to planting them in the ground: Build up a mound, spread the roots over it, fill in with soil, water thoroughly. (See illustrations on pages 137 and 167.)

**Planting annuals** or a mix of annuals plus a perennial or two is also not much different from putting them into a garden bed, except that you will put them much closer together. Fill up the container to within two inches from the top,

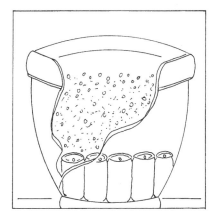 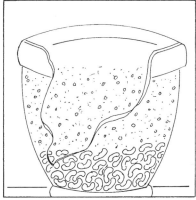

*To reduce the weight of very large containers, fill in some of the space with empty soda cans (left) or foam peanuts. Most flowers don't need the full depth of soil.*

slide the plants from their nursery packs, and gently loosen the roots. (See illustrations on pages 133 and 134.) Make a small crater with a trowel or your hand, fit the root ball down in, and fill in with soil.

---

### Planting Tip

If some of your plants are designed to tumble over the edge of the container, help them get started in the right direction by planting them near the edge and partly on their side, pointing outward.

---

## Maintaining Your Containers

Keeping your container garden looking sharp requires all the same routine maintenance you would need in a larger garden—but more often. Remember that containers are very concentrated landscapes, and they are in all likelihood positioned where people will look at them closely. You don't have the benefit of far-away vistas to disguise grungy-looking plants.

In particular, you have to be vigilant about pruning and tidying up, about fertilizing, and most especially about watering.

### PRUNING AND DEADHEADING

Pruning for shape is important if you have a shrub or small tree you want to keep at a modest size. It is also important if you're growing flowering annuals that tend to get leggy, with lots of plain stem and flowers only down at the tip end. The only solution is to keep them pinched back (see page 92), so they develop side growth and more flower buds. You have to do this on a regular basis, if you want constant bloom.

Sometimes, at the downside of the season or after a very hot spell, you can rejuvenate plants that seem to be bloomed out. Cut them back very severely, almost to the soil line, and keep watering and fertilizing them. It may take two or three weeks, but chances are good you'll get a whole new set of flowers.

### FERTILIZING

To keep annuals flowering, you need to put them on a program of regular fertilizing. This is doubly, triply true with containers. The problem is that with all the watering you're doing, you are dissolving away the nutrients in the potting soil, so they need to be replaced.

*If water runs right through when you water your container (left), that means the soil is completely dry—a serious problem. Loosen it all around with a sharp tool (right) and water slowly.*

Adding the time-release granules described on page 62 will help, but they are not sufficient by themselves. For the very showiest results, supplement with a weak solution of liquid fertilizer—one-quarter strength—about once a week.

Use a compete and balanced fertilizer (see Fertilizer chapter) with a higher proportion of phosphorus (the middle number). A lot of people like Miracle Gro, which is 15/30/15, for this.

### WATERING

The problem is not that container plants somehow need more water than other plants, but that the soil in the containers dries out faster. They do not have the buffer of surrounding soil in the rest of the garden to draw water from, or nearby lawn or ground cover to hold in moisture. Containers are surrounded by nothing but air. If that air is very hot or windy, or worst of all if it is both, it will pull the moisture out of the container faster than you can say Jack Robinson.

You have to face this: Growing in containers means being careful about water. In very hot weather, you will probably have to water every day. If you can't make that commitment, you might as well not even bother.

One sure sign that you have a problem is that the water runs right through immediately when you add it; that means the soil is so dried out it has pulled away from the sides of the container. Emergency action is needed: use something sharp to break up the dried soil, and then slowly add water. Best of all: If you can

*A container set down inside another container creates a space for an insulation layer (bark chips are used here) that will help prevent water loss and overheating.*

lift it, set the entire container down inside a larger container filled with water; hold it down until the soil is saturated (until air bubbles stop).

Here's one way to buy yourself a little insurance: set your container down inside a larger container and fill in the gap with bark dust or sphagnum moss. This extra layer of insulation will help protect your plant from very high temperatures and from the drying effect of wind. You can also make your life a bit easier by using the new self-watering containers. However, they merely buy you time, and they too need to be watered eventually. Neither of these approaches frees you from your basic responsibility: pay attention to your plants.

## Window Boxes

Even if you have no place to put an outdoor container—no patio, no balcony, no front stairs—I'll bet you can add a window box. For sweet, old-fashioned charm, nothing beats them. How about a container of culinary herbs outside your kitchen window? What could be more convenient?

• The box itself can be made from any of the materials described in this chapter (plastic, wood, terra cotta) but as with any container it must have a drainage hole.

- Use a good potting mix (for just one box, it may be easier to buy a bag than mix up your own).
- Notice sun patterns on your window; do you have full shade, part shade, morning sun, or afternoon sun? Choose plants accordingly.
- If you have a choice of windows, use the one that's closest to your water source.

Choosing the plants for a window box is in some ways the easiest of any kind of container because it is more limited—you cannot grow trees or shrubs in a window box. Select at least some plants that hang. A very nice combination uses three tiers: a trailing foliage plant (green or variegated) at the bottom, then cascading plants with colorful flowers, then a rank of smallish upright flowers.

In such a small space, related colors are generally more pleasing to the eye than several contrasting colors, which can look jittery and discordant. And keep in mind the backdrop against which the windowbox will be viewed. What is the basic color of the building? The window trim? Any shutters on the windows? Curtains visible through the window? The colors of the flowers should fit into the overall color scheme.

---

### Top 10 Annuals for Hanging Baskets or Window Boxes

1. Fuchsia. Trailing varieties, 12 to 24 inches. Colors white through all pinks, purples, and reds.
2. Lobelia. Trailing varieties, 10 to 12 inches. Colors white, blue, and rose.
3. Butterfly flower, "Poor man's orchid" (*Schizanthus*). 8 to 12 inches; spectacular, multicolor flowers.
4. Ivy-leaf geranium. Trail to 24 inches or more. Colors white, pink, and red.
5. Lotus vine. Frothy foliage trails 24 inches or more; flowers in red or yellow.
6. Lamium 'Silver Beacon.' Foliage is silver/green, trails to 3 feet. Insignificant pink or white flowers.
7. Petunia. Astonishing variety: single and double flowers in white, yellow, all shades of pink, red, and purple, and multicolors. Keep them pinched back.
8. Pansies. Trail to 12 inches. Unlimited color range, even black.
9. Impatiens. Semi-trailing, spreading mounds 18 to 24 inches. Colors white through pink/red/orange range; shade lover.
10. Tagetes marigolds. Bushy, lacy foliage spreading 12 to 18 inches. Flowers in yellows and oranges.

---

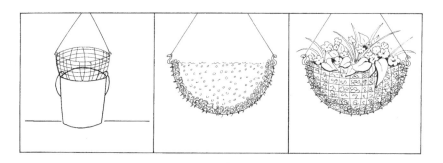

*Planting a wire hanging basket. Set the basket inside a bucket, for stability. Then line it with very wet sphagnum moss and fill in with rich potting soil (center), and you're ready to add the plants. Eventually these will grow over the edge and dangle down.*

## Hanging Baskets

Hanging containers allow you to double your garden area by taking advantage of air space. On balconies and patios, you'll need something to hang the containers from. Look around for places where you can add a hook or a large bracket. If you have the carpentry skills and the landlord's permission, you might add a cross-piece high above the balcony rail or a criss-cross shade structure to your patio, and hang containers from them.

If you have a full outdoor garden, you can also hang flower containers from tree limbs.

Containers for hanging are of two general types: (1) solid exterior and (2) open-grid. Both usually come with wires and a hook for hanging. Plant the solid ones just as you would any other container. The open grid type may be new to you. First fill all around the inner edge with a thick layer of sphagnum moss that you have presoaked. Then add planting mix as usual, and plant your plants.

Hanging containers present some challenges:

- If they are a large enough size to make an attractive planting, they will be heavy. You need to be careful where and how you hang them.
- Because they are often smaller than ground-level containers, it is even more critical that you water them faithfully. On the other hand, they can be harder to reach, and therefore it's tempting to get lazy about watering them. Be vigilant.
- If your area is small, think carefully about where to hang the containers and how high. You want them to be at optimal viewing level, but you don't want your friends walking into them.

*A*ll good gardens, including the ones that look as though they grew all on their own, rest on an invisible scaffolding of intelligent design. Making a great garden begins with understanding how colors work together, how shapes combine to establish balance, and how repetition and contrast unite to create rhythm. You must learn to see your garden with an artist's eye . . . except that because plants change their appearance as the seasons turn and the years progress, the garden/artist, unlike the painter or the architect, must design with the extra dimension of time.

No need to run to the nearest art class. If you have picked up this book you already possess the greatest assets for a designer: enthusiasm, appreciation of beauty, and a good head on your shoulders.

## Two Types of Design

Garden designs cluster into two large categories: formal and informal. Formal designs are rigidly symmetrical, are built on rectangular lines, and tend to include structural features such as statuary or fountains. Informal designs are asymmetrical, feature curved lines, and showcase plants rather than man-made structures. Most Americans seem to prefer informal gardens.

## The Building Blocks of Design

Whether formal or informal, all well-designed gardens reflect rhythm, balance, and unity of theme. You achieve those qualities by taking into account the physical properties of plants as you think about how to combine them—

because that's all garden design is: combining plants in pleasing ways. Think of the physical properties of the plants as the building blocks of garden design. The most important ones are:

- color
- shape
- texture
- size

## COLOR

Color is such a dominant element in how we experience gardens, and has such powerful emotional connections, it requires our greatest attention.

Take a look at the color wheel on page 51. It will help you appreciate why some colors clash and others combine beautifully.

- Complementary colors—directly across from each other on the wheel—look good together.
    Blue and orange.
    Yellow and violet (purple).
    Red and green.
- Colors on the same side of the color wheel are harmonious.
- Noncomplementary colors on opposite sides of the wheel can clash.

In nature, seldom do we see truly pure colors; more often they are shades or tints with undertones of an adjacent color. This is where the finesse of combining colors comes into play. For example, a shade of red with blue undertones will not look nearly as good next to yellow as would a red with orange undertones.

Blue, green, and purple are the cool colors. Red, orange, and yellow are warm colors. Cool colors recede, warm colors advance. That is to say, if we placed them on a hypothetical baseline, warm colors will seem closer and cool colors farther away. Use this to create the illusion of more space (or less, if a small, intimate garden is your goal). Cool colors will make a small garden seem larger; warm colors will make a large area seem smaller.

Another aspect of color is its power over us. Countless experiments by psychologists have demonstrated that cool colors are calming and warm colors are stimulating. Take a minute to think about how you want to experience your garden and the emotional environment you hope to create (a serene oasis, or a lively spot for entertaining), and plan your colors accordingly.

Here are some general approaches to building a design around color:

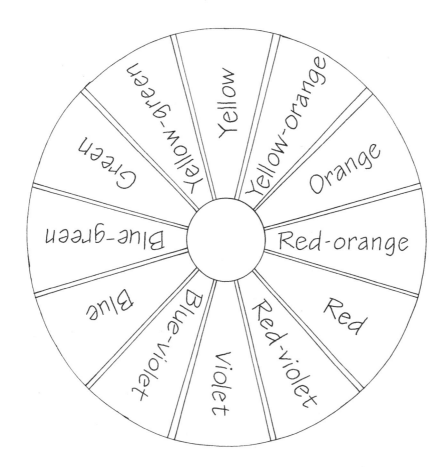

*Colors directly opposite each other on the color wheel are complementary. Colors that touch each other on the wheel look good together.*

1. *A monochrome garden*—all white flowers, for example, or the many shades of pink. It takes great discipline to maintain such a scheme, but the results are quite dramatic.
2. *Analagous*—using colors that are neighbors on the wheel. This is a surefire way to get compatible colors, as long as you don't have undertones that clash.
3. *Complementary*—built around colors that are each other's complement on the wheel.
4. *A combined approach*—analagous colors are the main theme, accented with carefully chosen complementary colors at certain points.

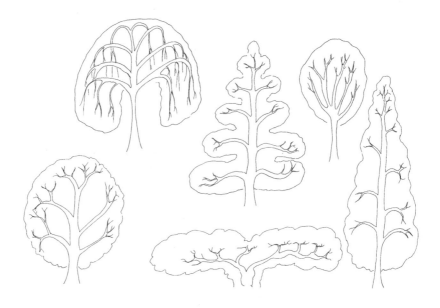

*Most trees (and many shrubs) assume one of these six basic shapes. (Top row, left to right): Weeping, pyramidal, vase-shaped. (Bottom row): rounded, spreading, columnar.*

### SHAPE

The element of shape is primarily a concern when planning placement of trees and shrubs. Because they are the largest elements in the landscape, and because they are present year-round, their shapes hold greater influence.

The main shapes for trees are:

| | |
|---|---|
| columnar | spreading |
| vase | weeping |
| rounded | pyramid |

Deciduous shrubs have these primary shapes:

| | |
|---|---|
| arching | rounded |
| erect | spreading |

Evergreen shrubs have these shapes:

| | |
|---|---|
| low and trailing | upright |
| spreading | round and compact |

Perennials and annuals have shape, too, of course, although often we are less conscious of this because it is the flowers themselves that command our attention. For convenience, we can think of them in the same terms as the basic shapes of trees and shrubs:

arching     rounded
upright     spreading

### TEXTURE

Garden designers have to think of texture on two levels:

1. The overall texture of the plant, best perceived when we are some distance away.
2. The texture of the foliage or flower, best perceived close up.

Overall texture is a function of such things as the branching pattern (open or dense), leaf size and shape (delicate or heavy), and density of foliage (lots of air or lots of leaves). Together, they create a total package that our eyes perceive as "soft," "coarse," "thick," "wispy," and so forth.

The actual surface texture of leaves (and, to a lesser extent, flowers) is more apparent when we are close to the plant. Leaves can be fuzzy, smooth, silky, coarse and leathery, frilly, etc. Leaves with different textures catch light in different ways, affecting the plants' visual impact. They also catch and hold water differently, adding another visual dimension.

### SIZE

For garden designers, the tricky part about size is that plants don't stay still. The only answer is to do your homework. Learn the mature size, both height and breadth, of the plants you're interested in. Also learn their rate of growth.

## Getting Down to Business

### DESIGN PRINCIPLES TO KEEP IN MIND:

- Group several of the same plant together; having just one of everything produces a jittery look.
- In groupings, odd numbers are more pleasing than even numbers. And a group in the shape of a triangle is more pleasing than plants in a straight line.

- A focal point in a garden can tie all the lines together. Focal points can be a beautiful tree or shrub, a structure such as a bench or gazebo, or a piece of sculpture.
- An open central area, such as a lawn, will make a small garden seem larger.
- A curving pathway leads you through the garden and entices with the hint of more to come.

### WHEN WORKING WITH COLOR, REMEMBER:

- Warm colors seem closer, cool colors seem farther away.
- Strong colors (like bright orange or very saturated yellow) jump out at you. In a small garden area, even a few of these bright flowers will dominate everything else. If you don't want that, surround them with something of an adjacent color and more pastel in hue to create a more gradual transition.
- Dark flowers against a dark background (such as a dark house or dark green trees) are hard to see.
- In a shady area, light-colored flowers or foliage will stand out better than darker ones.
- Bright, rich colors look good against a light-colored wall or fence.
- Warm colors will overwhelm nearby cool colors. If you have both in a small area, put hot colors at the back.
- Plants with gray or silver foliage or white flowers create a dramatic background for strong colors.
- Annuals often have deeply saturated colors; perennials, generally speaking, tend toward the pastel.

### WITH TEXTURE, REMEMBER:

- Contrast in texture is more interesting than planting all of the same texture.
- To make a small area seem larger, place small, bold plants in front and tall, delicate ones in back.
- You have to think of texture in conjunction with size. A low-growing ground cover with small glossy leaves has a delicate texture, and so does a Japanese maple, but the maple will provide better contrast for a hedge of evergreen shrubs.

### WITH SHAPE, REMEMBER:

- Unless you're going for a very formal effect, using all the same shape is boring.
- Tall slender trees and shrubs lead the eye upward; weeping trees and shrubs lead the eye downward. In your planning, consider what's at the end of that sight line.
- Flowers have shape as well as color: they can be tall and spiky, shaped like round balls, in drooping clusters, have small individual flowers forming a free-form mass, and so on.

- Size doesn't exist in a vacuum. The right size tree for your front yard is the one that relates best to the size of your house and the total landscape.
- Intelligent contrast contributes rhythm, but too great a contrast in size is unsettling: a few tiny alpine plants under humongous fir trees look silly.
- Our perception of size is affected by texture. A 20-foot aspen tree and a 20-foot spruce, because of their very different texture, seem to take up different amounts of space, even though both are 20 feet tall.

## *Putting It on Paper*

Converting these principles into reality is what making a garden is all about. That process will be far smoother if you first sketch out your ideas on paper. It is a great deal simpler to move trees around on a drawing pad than in real life.

*Planning a new garden on paper saves a lot of headaches later on. The garden plot was measured and sketched out on graph paper, and plant combinations were roughed in. Now color cutouts from mail-order catalogs, taped on the layout, will verify that plants do (or do not) look good together.*

DESIGNING

YOUR

GARDEN

| PLANT | SUN NEEDS | BLOOMS WHEN | COLOR | HEIGHT | WIDTH | SPECIAL TRAITS |
|---|---|---|---|---|---|---|
| | | | | | | |
| | | | | | | |
| | | | | | | |
| | | | | | | |
| | | | | | | |
| | | | | | | |

Begin by developing a rough list of plants you are considering for your space. Let's assume for the moment that you have a few books from the library and a hefty collection of mail-order catalogs that you borrowed from a friend. Browse through them and start building your list. Then add in the factor of growing conditions: will the items on your tentative list do well in the particular garden spot you are planning?

Many people find it helpful to construct a list or matrix chart, such as the one on page 56.

## Make a Model

A very good way to preview the look of your garden areas is to make a two-dimensional model, using the cut-and-paste method (see page 55). Here's what you need:

1. All the mail-order catalogs you can get your hands on
2. Scissors, glue or tape
3. Blank sheets of paper

Sketch out the rough dimensions of your garden plot; draw in big blobs to show where different plants will go. Now cut out pictures of the plants you're considering and place them on the drawing. Move them around until you like the results, then glue them in place. Sometimes you will have to mentally fill in what the photos do not show: What about leaf texture? What about final size (spread and height)?

> **Shortcut:** Several mail-order nurseries have already designed a garden for you, with names like "Sunny Perennial Border." When you order this package deal, you get a garden layout, planting instructions, and all the plants.

**FERTILIZER**

*A*lthough you will hear people say they are "feeding" their plants when they add fertilizer, in actuality plants manufacture their own food, in the process known as photosynthesis. The raw materials for that manufacturing process come from the air and from the soil. If the soil does not have an adequate supply of those raw materials—nutrients—the plants do not thrive, so those nutrients must be added to the soil in some form or other.

That's what fertilizer is—a replacement source of essential nutrients.

## What's in Fertilizer?

The three main nutrients for all plants, the ones they use the most of, are:

1. Nitrogen, chemical symbol N
2. Phosphorus, P
3. Potassium, K

When you purchase fertilizer, the package will display its formula of those three as a set of three numbers, in this order: N, P, K.

The three numbers on the label do not add up to 100; that would produce fertilizer of such a strong concentration that it would burn the plants. The rest is made up of inert filler, along with perhaps minor nutrients and trace elements.

It is easier to compare different brands and formulations of fertilizer if you think of the numbers as a ratio. Seen that way, 5/5/5, 10/10/10, and 20/20/20 formulations are all the same; they're all 1/1/1 ratios. The difference is that you would have to use four times as much of the 5/5/5 product to get the same oomph as the 20/20/20 product, and at greater cost per unit.

Nitrogen stimulates growth and development of chlorophyll (the green substance in leaves that photosynthesis

*All fertilizer packages, both organic and synthetic, display three numbers, representing percentage by volume of the three primary nutrients for plants. The first number is always nitrogen, then phosphorus, then potassium.*

depends on). Phosphorus provides growth energy for new plants and then helps them develop flowers. Potassium, in a way not yet fully understood, builds strong root systems and promotes overall hardiness.

As a very broad generalization, we can say that:

- Nitrogen is for the foliage and stems.
- Phosphorus is for flowers (and therefore fruit).
- Potassium is for roots.

Thus, if your main concern is with flowers, choose a fertilizer with a higher middle number; if you want to promote lush green foliage, you need a higher first number.

---

### Fertilizer Rules of Thumb

Keeping in mind the idea of ratio, rather than absolute numbers, here are some broad guidelines for fertilizer formulas.

| | |
|---|---|
| Vegetables | 1/1/1 (or 1/2/1 for fruiting vegetables with a long growing period, like tomatoes and peppers) |
| Annual flowers | 1/2/1 |
| Flowering perennials | 1/2/1 |
| Foliage perennials | 1/1/1 |
| Roses | 1/2/1 |
| Lawn, newly seeded | 1/2/1 |
| Lawn, existing | 5/1/2 |
| Shrubs | 1/1/1 |
| Flowering shrubs | 1/2/1 |
| Trees | 1/1/1 |
| Flowering trees | 1/2/1 |
| Houseplants | 2/1/1 |

---

In addition to the Big Three, commercial fertilizer may contain the following secondary nutrients and trace elements.

- Sulfur. It works with nitrogen to make plant cells. Often deficient in soils in areas where it rains a lot.
- Calcium. Important for cell growth; the plant takes it in through the roots, so it must be in the soil right by the root tips.
- Magnesium. Essential component of chlorophyll.
- Trace elements: iron, zinc, manganese, copper, and others. Each is important, but plants need only tiny amounts.

---

### Tip: Magnesium

An easy and inexpensive source of magnesium is epsom salts, from the drugstore. Mix in 1 pound for an area of 200 square feet.

---

Nutrient deficiency may be the culprit if your plants are not growing well and you have already checked all the obvious things. It can be difficult, however, to pinpoint just which nutrient is missing. If you had a soil analysis done (see Soil chapter), and it revealed a deficiency in any nutrient, you will want to search out a fertilizer that provides the deficient nutrient. Most of the time, a good all-around fertilizer will provide the minute amounts of these trace nutrients that your plants need.

As if all that wasn't confusing enough, you will also find on the shelves of your favorite garden center a number of fertilizers formulated for specific kinds of plants. There is fertilizer for roses, rhododendrons, vegetables, tomatoes, lawns, houseplants, orchids, and heaven knows what else. But if you look closely, you'll see that the real difference among them is the proportion each has of the three main nutrients.

# Types of Fertilizer

The terms used to describe fertilizer can be confusing, so let's take a minute for a basic rundown.

- *Complete* fertilizer has all three main nutrients, in some proportion.
- *Balanced* fertilizer has all three nutrients in relatively equal proportion (8–10–7, or 10–10–10).

---

### Organic Fertilizers

Here are the proportionate ingredients of some common organic fertilizers:

| | |
|---|---|
| Cottonseed meal | 7/3/2 |
| Bonemeal | 2/25/0 |
| Bloodmeal | 13/2/1 |
| Fishmeal | 10/7/0 |
| Soybean meal | 7/2/2 |
| Wood ashes | 0/2/5 |
| Seaweed | 2/1/15 |
| Superphoshate | 0/20/0 |
| Potash sulfate | 0/0/48 |

Manure varies in nutrient content depending on what kind of animal it was and what foods it was fed. Usually, the nutrient value overall is low, with more nitrogen than phosphorus or potassium.

---

FERTILIZER

- *Incomplete* fertilizer has two of the three.
- *Simple* fertilizer has just one of the three.

As a consumer, you may be more interested in the different physical forms fertilizer comes in:

- Dry granules that you mix with water before adding to the plants.
- Dry powder that you work into the soil as is, without dilution.
- Liquid fertilizer that you dilute with water.
- Time-release granules that you work into the soil. These are small pellets of fertilizer, about the size of small BBs, encased in a coating that slowly dissolves when coming into contact with water, so that the fertilizer is gradually released over time.
- Short spikes of compacted fertilizer that you insert into the soil next to the plants. This is also a gradual-release formula, especially popular and convenient with houseplants.

### ORGANIC OR INORGANIC?

Organic fertilizer is made from something that was once alive. Inorganic fertilizer is made from synthetic materials. Bonemeal, fish fertilizer (made from decomposed dead fish), commercially packaged manure (made from you-know-what)—those are all forms of organic fertilizer. In addition, there are commercial manufacturers of organic fertilizer; their products are packaged just like the inorganic types, and usually proudly proclaim "organic" on the label.

Is one better than the other? Both have their loyal supporters. Those who prefer organic fertilizer generally favor environmentally sensitive practices in all aspects of their lives. Fans of synthetic fertilizer usually claim that it is faster and more dependable, and they are at least partially right: most organics release their nutrients slowly. The flip side is, they stay in the soil longer. Another of life's pesky tradeoffs. If you can embrace both mindsets, using both types, alternately, will give you a full range of long- and short-term benefits.

---

### The First Law of Fertilizer:

Follow manufacturer's directions. Do not use a stronger concentration. You'll only burn your plants.

---

*A* ground cover is a substitute for a lawn. (Actually, a lawn *is* a ground cover, but in the world of gardening the term usually means other-than-lawn.) It is what you use if you want to blanket an area with something but you don't want, or for some reason can't grow, a lawn. Ground covers are not maintenance-free, but they are a great deal less work than a lawn.

Ground covers are very popular with landscapers who design and maintain commercial spaces like the grounds of an office building or an industrial park. In home gardens, they are excellent solutions to two very common problems:

1. A sloping terrain that would be difficult or even dangerous to mow. (In addition to their esthetic virtues, ground covers also hold the soil in place, preventing erosion.)
2. Areas underneath trees and shrubs where grass won't grow because of shade and competition from tree roots, or where it's too difficult to get a lawnmower.

How one defines what makes a ground cover is largely a matter of interpretation. Basically, it's any planting of one specific plant, massed together so thickly that no bare dirt shows through and weeds have no place to call home. There is a fundamental assumption that the plants are low to the ground; a bed of rhododendrons would not be considered ground cover, no matter how close together they were.

## Types of Ground Covers

**Perennials** present the widest variety. There are many wonderful and charming plants that multiply readily, spreading out in all directions. Either they spread from underground runners, or they set roots wherever a growing node touches the ground. In either case, they will completely take over an area, so think carefully where you put them. If you don't want them spreading into an adjoining flower bed, you'll need some kind of physical barrier; otherwise, be prepared to keep yanking them out. This rampant growth also means that you should thin the plants every year, once they are fully established.

A particularly nice feature of perennial ground covers is that most of them flower. Some perennial ground covers are evergreen, but most behave like other perennials: die back in winter, come up again in spring.

**Shrubs** may be evergreen or deciduous. Many evergreen ground covers are special varieties of conifers that have been bred for their habit of growing close to the ground. A very common one is juniper.

Deciduous ground covers are shrubs that have a horizontal growth habit; they grow out sideways rather than upward. A familiar example, and a very beautiful one, is *Cotoneaster horizontalis*. In cooler climates they lose leaves in the winter. This is not as awful as it might at first sound; weeds don't usually grow during the winter. (But you will have to be alert in the spring, when the weeds and renegade clumps of grass may try to get a foothold before the ground covers are fully leafed out.)

Both types need regular pruning so they will grow tight and dense, rather than long and straggly; see Pruning chapter for details.

**Vines** spread every which way, rooting all along the stems as they grow. In other words, they become very firmly established wherever they are. If you should ever decide you want to take them out, you have a devil of a job on your hands. The most mild-mannered people turn snarly trying to rip out old ivy. (And by the way, do be careful with ivy; if it starts to grow around the trunk of a tree, the tree's a goner.)

# Planting a Ground Cover

At the nursery, you will find ground covers in containers of varying size: one-gallon pots, four-inch pots, and flats (big shallow boxes planted with just one type of plant).

Planting the baby plants is like planting anything else (see the Container section of the chapter on Planting), except that you must plan to incorporate a mulch. It is going to take a while for the plants to reach a large enough size to completely cover the ground. In the meantime, you have to cover up the gaps, or you have defeated the purpose of a ground cover.

You can cover up the gaps with a thick layer of bark chips, in which case you must be prepared to keep after the weeds until the plants get bigger, or you can use black plastic. If you opt for the plastic, you must put it down before planting.

1. Prepare the soil for planting. (See chapters on Soil and Planting.)
2. Cover the area with plastic (let's assume for the moment you are using it). At the recommended spacing (see below) cut an X in the plastic and fold back the points to expose the soil; the size of the X will depend on the size of your plants.
3. Meanwhile, water the flat or containers thoroughly.
4. Use a hand trowel to dig a hole where the X was cut. Separate the plants and plant one in each hole. Water each plant and let it drain while you move on to the next one.
5. Fold the points of the X back around the plants, and hide the plastic under a layer of bark dust.

Now, here's where people who hate black plastic *really* hate it. As the ground cover plants grow and fill in, it gets harder and harder to get in between them—that is, after all, the whole idea. Eventually the plastic will develop rips, and you will want to remove it, which is difficult to do because it is covered with bark chips and the plants are in the way. You may wish you had just used bark mulch in the first place.

## SPACING

How far apart you space the individual plants depends on how quickly they grow and how large they are when you plant them. Ground covers that are low-growing forms of shrubs (juniper, for instance) are generally spaced 3 to 4 feet apart. Most one-gallon plants are in the range of 18 to 24 inches. Plants in four-inch pots are spaced anywhere from 12 to 20 inches, depending on how rapidly the plants grow. Plants grown in flats (such as periwinkle or ivy) are set at 10 to 12 inches, generally.

*a* hedge is a row of plants, usually in a straight line, deliberately placed to form a barrier, a screen, or a backdrop. When you hear someone refer to a "hedge plant," that's not a certain species but a specific usage. It could be any of a number of different species.

Most hedge plants are shrubs—which means that hedges can be deciduous or evergreen; can be tall, medium, or short; can have green or variegated foliage; can have berries or not . . . all the esthetic qualities you would consider when selecting shrubs as a design element in your garden should also be in your thoughts as you choose shrubs for hedges.

And you will have to decide early on whether you want a formal or informal hedge. Formal means that the plants are kept trimmed into a boxy shape; informal means they are allowed to assume their own natural shape with only light pruning to keep them in bounds. Neither is inherently better than the other; this is purely a question of personal taste and the overall style of your garden.

In addition, you will also be thinking about the purpose that you want the hedge to achieve.

## The Right Hedge for the Purpose

Let me emphasize: many, many kinds of plants work as hedges, including quite a few you might never have thought about. Which you choose has everything to do with your reason for putting up a hedge in the first place.

Some of the more common reasons are:

- To provide a privacy screen.
- To block a view that you don't like.
- To serve as a windbreak.
- To absorb street noise.

- To control foot traffic, preventing unwanted shortcuts across the lawn, for instance.
- To serve as a green fence, keeping pets or small children in or out.
- To create a green backdrop—for other plants, for sculpture, for a sundial, for a gazebo, for . . . whatever.
- To outline a path or walkway, guiding the eye and the visitor in the intended direction.

### Top 12 Hedge Plants

1. Privet. Small-leaf evergreen; one of the old standbys. Fast grower. Old hedges can be cut to the ground and will regrow.
2. Laurel. Large-leaf evergreen. Fast grower reaches huge heights if not pruned; for large areas only.
3. Arborvitae. Evergreen with cedar-like foliage. Slow growing, very dense, excellent for privacy and easy maintenance.
4. Azalea. Evergreen, low profile, slow growing, brilliant spring flower display.
5. Boxwood. Small-leaf evergreen, both dwarf and standard varieties, slow to medium growth. Another old standby.
6. Juniper. Several varieties have a shrubby profile. Slow growing, easy to maintain.
7. Photinia. Resembles laurel but of a more restrained size. New growth is rich red or bronze, depending on variety. Fast growing, requires frequent pruning to keep in good shape and display desirable colored foliage. Not for the "once a year" pruner.
8. English yew. This is the plant used for England's famous hedges. Evergreen, medium growth, easy to maintain.
9. Abelia. Semi-evergreen, both dwarf and standard varieties. Small heart-shaped leaves with reddish cast, profuse pink flowers. Fast grower but prunes well; very graceful.
10. Leyland cypress. Evergreen with bluish-green foliage and a weeping habit. Makes a very large hedge.
11. Cotoneaster. Numerous varieties, both evergreen and semi-evergreen. Fast grower, with wonderful red or orange berries nearly all year.
12. Japanese andromeda (*Pieris*). Evergreen in most zones. Slow grower. New growth is red; clusters of small pink or white blooms in late winter or early spring. Light pruning stimulates attractive new growth.

Choosing the proper plant for your purpose depends largely on common sense. If you don't want to be able to see what's on the other side of the hedge, or for other people to see in, then you must choose hedge plants that have dense foliage all the way down to the ground, and obviously you want them to be evergreen.

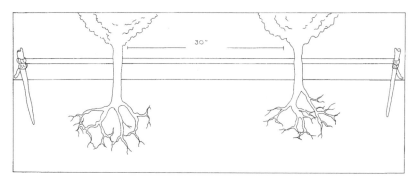

*To make sure you plant a new hedge in a straight line, tie string between stakes. To get even spacing, measure the recommended distance on the string and tie on short lengths of colored thread at that point.*

If you want to keep people from cutting across your yard, or keep toddlers and pets from wandering off, you need something that has thorns or brambles. (Shrub roses make a lovely hedge.)

If you want a backdrop, and you want it to be the same all the time, it should be evergreen. If seasonal changes would enhance your backdrop, you can choose deciduous plants.

Hedges used as landscape elements, providing a backdrop for other plants, can be—and should be—visually integrated into the whole.

Size is a consideration too. If you want to use hedges to outline the path to the front door, choose something that stays small; a high hedge used this way would create a tunnel, which is not a welcoming feeling. Similarly, a hedge along your property line needs to be tall if your goal is to screen out your neighbors, and short if you want to define the border but encourage contact.

# Planting and Caring for Hedges

The plants you purchase for your new hedge may come bareroot, in a container, or balled-and-burlapped. The basic planting process is the same as that described in the chapter on Planting. What you have to be careful about with hedges is making sure you maintain a straight line (assuming a straight line is what you want).

First mark out the line with stakes and string, as shown in the illustration on

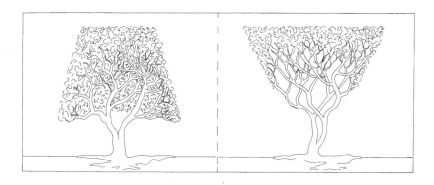

*The correct way to prune a formal hedge (left) lets air and light to the bottom layer. The wrong way (right) blocks light from the lower branches, creating a bare bottom.*

the previous page. Then plant as usual. Most should be spaced 2 to 3 feet apart, depending on how large the plants get when they reach full size. For a tight, formal hedge using something like arborvitae, 2 to 2¹/₂ foot spacing is best; for a less formal look (with a freeform shrub), 3 to 3¹/₂ feet might work better.

If you have chosen deciduous plants or broadleaf evergreens, prune them just above a node just after planting, so they will branch out and grow into full, dense plants. Next spring, cut all branches back by one third. That way, you'll get fast, dense growth.

Once your plants have grown to a good size (or if you inherited a mature hedge from the previous owner), you must keep the hedge trimmed, if a formal style is what you have chosen. Hedge clippers are a necessity for this operation, either manual (illustrated on page 154) or power-assisted. Whichever you do, follow the main rule of pruning hedges:

> ### The First Law of Pruning Hedges:
> Make the bottom of the plant wider than the top, not the other way around.

The reason is simple: if the top is wider than the bottom, it will keep light from reaching the lower branches and they will not grow well. Eventually the bottom tier will die out, and you'll have ugly bare spots.

Note in the Top 10 list that some hedge plants grow faster than others. This is obviously a good thing if you are starting from scratch, but realize it also means that regular pruning becomes a part of your life forever.

**HERBS**

*I*f you're feeling a bit nervous about gardening, not sure how and where to get started, have I got good news for you: growing herbs is *easy*. Honest. Herbs are easy because:

- They will grow quite nicely in less than perfect soil.
- They don't get many diseases.
- Bugs don't bother them very much, because they don't like the taste.
- They're not picky about water.
- You don't have to worry much about pruning; it happens naturally when you snip off pieces of the plants to use.
- Most of them are perennials, and even most of the annuals are self-seeding.

On top of all that, there is the great satisfaction of growing something that is so useful and enriches our lives in so many ways: enhancing the flavor of foods; healing our common ailments; providing materials for potpourri and other flower crafts, for dyes, and for natural household and beauty products.

Marvelous, aromatic plants that are easy to grow and give us a great deal in return—it's easy to see why herbs and herb gardening have become so very popular in recent years.

## Planning Your Herb Garden

You do not need a full-fledged herb garden to experience the joys of fresh herbs. You can slip individual herb plants here and there in your garden, wherever you have an empty spot. Most of them are quite pretty, and many have nice, gentle flowers. I highly recommend this approach, especially if you're just getting started with herbs.

You do not even need a garden. Apartment dwellers can grow a miniature herb garden in a container or window box. See the chapter on Containers for a few suggestions.

## Top 10 Herbs

1. Basil. Annual, very tender. For cooking. Lots of wonderful varieties, with undertones of lemon, cinnamon, and cloves, and deep purple leaves as well as all colors of green.
2. Chamomile. Annual (German) or perennial (Roman). Low-growing, covered with tiny daisylike flowers. Dried flowers make very soothing tea.
3. Fennel. Perennial or self-sowing annual. The fat base is eaten like a vegetable, the seeds are used as a spice, and the beautiful feathery foliage makes a glorious garnish. All parts of the plant taste like licorice.
4. Lavender. Perennial. For its exquisite, old-fashioned fragrance.
5. Mint. Perennial. Probably the easiest plant in the whole world to grow, mint comes in lots of amazing varieties: chocolate, peppermint, apple, orange, pineapple, and many more. You have to have it for tea, and for mint juleps.
6. Oregano. Perennial. Soft magenta flowers. Can't make spaghetti sauce without it.
7. Rosemary. Perennial, somewhat tender. Tiny blue flowers hug the stem.
8. Sage. Perennial. Beautiful mounded shape enhances any landscape; taste enhances Thanksgiving turkey. Comes with variegated foliage: yellow/green, cream/pink/green.
9. Tarragon. Perennial. A small, unassuming little plant with a knockout taste.
10. Thyme. Perennial. Low-growing creeper, nice in rock gardens. Comes in an astonishing array of varieties: lemon, lime, cinnamon, apple, orange, nutmeg, caraway, and a million others.

In all cases, you start the same way you start planning any garden: asking yourself what you want, and what you have to work with. That is to say, start by envisioning how you would be using herbs:

- in cooking
- to make your own herbal tea
- in scented crafts and gifts such as potpourri
- to make nontoxic household products (such as flea or moth repellents), natural cosmetics or natural dyes

Then decide which particular herbs might you want for that purpose. (This might take a little research; as with any garden, you read a bit, look at plants, doodle a bit.) For instance:

- If you like potpourri, you might enjoy growing lavender and lemon verbena.
- If you would like to make your own herbal tea blend, maybe you'll want to grow spearmint, chamomile, and lemon balm.

- If culinary herbs are your goal, take a minute and think about which herbs you most like to cook with.

Next, consider the esthetic qualities of the plants: size, shape, leaf color and texture, flower color, and so on. As much as possible, you'll want to place the herbs where they blend well with the plants nearby.

Then do a bit of homework and learn what growing conditions your favorite herbs prefer. With herbs it's easier than with many other types of plants because the great majority of them like full sun and few are picky about soil. If you take my suggestion and start off by integrating herb plants into the rest of your garden, all you really have to do is look for a bare spot somewhere in the sun, and plunk one in.

---

### Herbs in the Shade

Most herbs prefer a sunny location. But there are a few that would rather be in the shade:

|  |  |
|---|---|
| angelica | chervil |
| sweet cicely | sweet woodruff |

---

## Herb Gardens

It won't be long, I'll bet, before you're ready to think about a full herb garden, planted just with herbs. You have many traditions, both old and modern, from which to draw inspiration for designs.

In essence, herb gardens take one of three shapes: circles, squares, or rectangles. The shapes are usually divided into smaller segments, as a way of separating one type of herb from another and to make cultivating, weeding, and harvesting easier. Two basic designs are suggested here (see pages 76 and 77). One virtue of both these designs is that they can easily be expanded, if your enthusiasm grows as fast as your herbs.

One design I would urge you not to attempt is the fanciful knot garden so often seen in photographs. These designs date from earlier centuries in Europe, at the estates of wealthy families who had an essential requirement most of us lack today: full-time gardeners on staff. These gardens are meant to be viewed from above (as from the upper windows of the castle) to fully appreciate the interlocking patterns, and require constant pruning to maintain the intricate shapes. Frankly, they're not worth the trouble.

# Growing Herbs

Perennial herbs are usually purchased as small container plants; plant them in the garden whenever the ground is workable (not frozen, not waterlogged); see Planting chapter. Annuals may also by purchased this way, or started from seed. If you do use seeds, you'll have better results if you start them indoors; this gives you a head start on the growing season. (See chapter on Seeds for how-to's.)

In terms of routine care, herbs do better if you give them only minimal attention. Let me explain the reason behind that heretical statement: The aroma and taste that we associate with herbs are carried in the plant's cells as essential oils. When an herb plant is given rich soil, lots of water, regular fertilizer, and all the rest, it grows big and lush. But the individual leaves are not proportionately lush in essential oils. When the plant grows more moderately, the essential oils are more concentrated. Think of it this way: Many of our more popular herbs are native to the Mediterranean—lavender, oregano, marjoram, rosemary, thyme, and savory, among others. In the dry, rocky soil of that region, they thrive.

Of course there are exceptions to this—there are always exceptions—but as a general rule we can say if you are growing an herb for its aroma or taste, those qualities will be more pronounced if the plant is given only a moderately rich environment. On the other hand, if you are more interested in the flowers for decorative purposes, or the herb plant as a landscape ingredient, then you want them to grow luxuriously, and you can water and fertilize the heck out of them.

The one thing you must pay attention to in all cases is adequate drainage; no plant will survive if its roots are in standing water, and most herbs are quite particular in this regard.

Also, all the annual herbs need more of your attention to ensure they have every opportunity in their short lives to do whatever it is you want from them. If you grow dill for the seed, the plant must grow strongly enough to make flowers and set seed before winter frost. Basil, that fabulous kitchen herb, is extremely tender; the leaves will turn black in an instant when the temperature starts dropping. So you must help it grow vigorously during the warm days, and harvest the leaves continuously to encourage more to follow. These popular herbs are all annuals:

| | |
|---|---|
| anise | basil |
| borage | calendula |
| German chamomile | coriander |
| dill | summer savory |

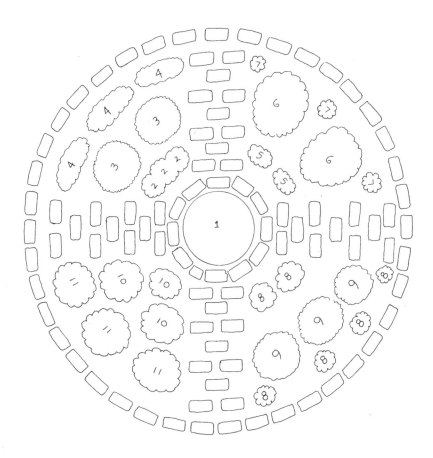

*Circular herb garden layout has a classic look. Bricks crossing through at right angles make it possible to reach all plants from all sides. On the layout, numbers indicating specific herbs correspond to plant list.*

### Biennial Herbs

A few herbs are biennial (live two years). If you let the seeds fall to the ground, you'll have perpetual plantings of:

        angelica
        caraway
        chervil (often treated as an annual)
        parsley

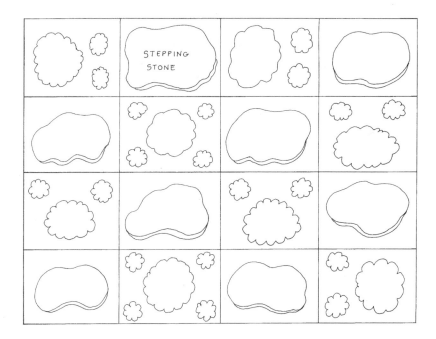

*Checkerboard-style layout is infinitely expandable. Small and large herbs alternate with stepping stones and will eventually grow to fill in all the gaps.*

# Pruning

Annual herbs don't need pruning in the traditional sense, but they do require constant pinching back (see page 92). Once a plant starts to flower, its leaves become rather bitter. So if the leaves are your goal—basil, for example—keep the flower heads pinched off.

Perennial herbs are pruned like other perennials in your garden. If the plants are herbaceous—die to the ground in winter, return in the spring—you don't have to do any pruning, but you may have to thin them after a few years. Examples include sweet woodruff, mint, tarragon, lovage, and bergamot.

Perennial plants with hard, woody stems (lavender, sage, rosemary, for example) do not die back in the winter; these are the ones that need pruning to keep them producing new leaves. Do it in early spring, before the plant starts showing new growth; cut back each main stem to about one-third or one-half its length. (Review general principles in the Pruning chapter before doing so.)

If someone (undoubtedly the homeowner before you) neglected to do this, the plant develops a scraggly center with bare stems and fresh leaves only at the top. You may be successful in rejuvenating the plant if you cut it back severely, almost to the ground, in early spring. Just be sure you leave some foliage, so the plant can continue to manufacture its food (see chapter on Fertilizer). One technique that works well is to do this in stages: one year, prune one half of the plant hard; leave the other half alone until next year. In the meantime the unpruned part will look awful; just close your eyes.

Warning: this does not always work. My feeling is, try it anyway; you have little to lose. The other course is to discard the plant and start anew.

## Winter Protection

There are comparatively few herb plants that need some special care in cold weather. The usual techniques are to heap a thick pile of mulch around the base of the plant, or cover it with burlap, or both. A simpler approach, I believe, since most herb plants are relatively small, is to move them to a protected area.

To do that you can either dig up the plant and put it in a container; or grow the plant in a container in the first place, and plan to move it to some shelter: closer to the house, to a back porch, or enclosed patio.

- Sweet bay and lemon verbena can stay outdoors only in very warm climates; gardeners in other regions grow them in pots, so they can easily move them to shelter in winter.
- Marjoram is only semihardy; many Northern gardeners grow it as an annual. It's also a good candidate for container growing.
- Rosemary will freeze in very cold weather, but it is hardier than the other three.

## Harvesting and Preserving Your Herbs

The essential oils that give herbs the qualities we want are most pronounced just before the plant is ready to flower. Those same oils are also dissipated by warm sunshine. Remember those two things, and you will always know when is the very best time to harvest:

*Before flowering, and early in the morning.*

However, I must say something here about herb flowers. They are quite pretty, in a soft, usually subtle way; even more important, they are very attractive to bees, which are critical to a healthy ecosystem. I like to leave some plants of each group to flower, both for myself and the bees. And of course, common sense says that if you are growing herbs for seeds (like dill or fennel), you must leave the flowers on the plant.

The process of harvesting could not be simpler: use your fingers or your pruners, and snip off sections of the plant. If you're going to use them in cooking immediately, cut off just enough for that one meal. Otherwise, it's easier to handle the next steps if you harvest larger pieces.

The classic way of preserving herbs is drying, but that is not your only option.

## DRYING

Once the moisture in the cells has evaporated, a plant's leaves, flowers, and stems will not rot. In that respect, dried materials will store indefinitely. However, dried herbs don't keep their *flavor* indefinitely; it's best to start anew each year.

The techniques used for drying depend somewhat on the type of plant, but the ideal surroundings are always the same. You want a spot where there is good air circulation but the atmosphere is warm and dry. Avoid rooms that are humid, if you have a choice, because it defeats your purpose.

Attics are usually terrific, if you have one. Otherwise, look up: the top of the refrigerator, on top of upper cabinets, and so forth. The higher the location in a room, the warmer the air there. A flower shop in my neighborhood has suspended a very large, completely flat wicker tray from the ceiling, high above people's heads. Whatever flowers don't sell go up there for drying. It works wonderfully.

The two basic techniques are:

1. *Spread the cuttings out flat.* You want something that lets air circulate but has small enough grids that things don't fall through. An old window screen is perfect. So are the racks from a food dehydrator (if you have one). For small amounts, you can use wicker trays, even paper towels spread out on the counter.

   All herbs can be dried this way, and this is the best choice for plants with very tiny leaves (thyme, tarragon, small-leafed basils, etc.). Spread out the whole stem, so nothing falls through the holes. Plants with larger leaves can be dried this way too; I prefer, though, to strip the leaves from the stem while they are still fresh, and scatter them over the drying rack.

2. *Suspend them from something.* Bundle several stems together, tie with string or rubber bands, and hang them upside down. Tie paper bags around the flower heads if you wish to collect the seeds.

   Possibilities for drying racks include: a curtain rod or dowel hung from the ceiling, a line of cup hooks on the ceiling, even a broom handle stretched

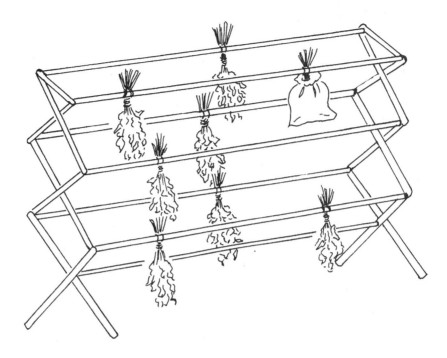

*Bundles of herbs dry in about a week; use paper bags to catch seeds of dill, fennel, coriander, and other seed herbs.*

over the backs of two chairs. My favorite is one of those collapsible racks intended for drying clothes; you can get a lot of herbs in a very small floor space.

In both cases, the leaves are ready when they are crunchy. That can take anywhere from two days to a week. Keep an eye on progress. It does no good to leave things on the drying rack collecting dust after they are well dried.

The flavor of dried herbs lasts longer if the leaves are left whole. That is why I remove leaves from the stem before drying whenever possible; you don't lose as much to crumbling that way. But it's practically impossible to do that with very tiny leaves, so I dry the whole stem as a unit and then strip them off once dry. On the other hand, whole dried leaves take up more space than crumbled ones. You have to decide this for yourself, based on your storage space.

The best containers for dried herbs are glass jars with a tight-fitting lid. Label each one with the name of the herb and the date, even if you think you can remember; all dried leafy herbs look alike. For best quality, store the containers away from

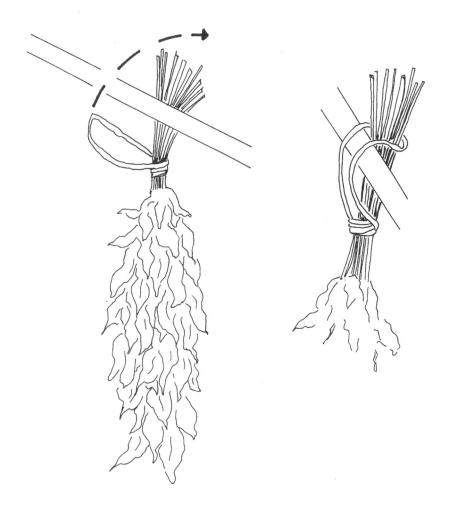

*Fasten bundles this quick and easy way with rubber bands, which continue to hold firmly even though stems shrink during drying.*

heat and light. Inside the refrigerator is perfect, if you have the room. Or in a cool cupboard. Just don't keep them right above the stove—it's way too hot.

Dried herbs significantly lose quality after a year. That's one of the great joys of growing your own herbs: you always have a replacement supply coming in.

### OTHER PRESERVING METHODS

Freezing works quite well for herbs; they turn black, but the flavor is retained very nicely. Here's how to do it:

First, make sure the leaves are very dry; if you rinsed them, or if they still have dew on them, let them air dry. Strip leaves from the stem, pack them loosely into pint freezer bags, and push out all the air. That's all there is to it.

---

### Herbs: A Few Surprises

1. Hyssop. Perennial. Pretty blue flowers, popular with bees and other beneficial insects. Very valuable if you also have a vegetable garden.
2. Catnip. Perennial. If you have a cat you know about catnip, but did you know you can grow it? And did you know it makes a very delicious, soothing tea for the cat's owner?
3. Bergamot. Perennial. Grow it for two reasons: (1) Leaves have a mild orange flavor; add them to regular black tea, and you have a homemade version of Earl Gray tea. (2) They have wonderful, funky red flowers, which, like all herb flowers, are edible.
4. Pineapple sage. Very tender perennial. It really is a sage, and it really tastes like pineapple. Use it in ham or chicken sauces, or dressing for fruit salad; makes wonderful tea. If not killed by frost, in late summer it produces the most astonishing flowers: bright red and shaped like a long trumpet.

---

Another version of freezing produces small blocks of herbs, enough for one dish. To make them, puree the herb leaves in the blender or food processor with a small amount of water; pour the slush into ice cube trays and freeze. Remove the frozen cubes from the tray and pack into freezer bags; to use, remove just one at a time, as needed. You can also put several herbs together in the blender, and produce cubes especially for spaghetti, for pot roast, for meatloaf, or whatever suits your tastebuds.

There's one more storage technique I use often. When you add herbs to some dish you're cooking, you also quite often add other things: oil, butter, or vinegar. Take advantage of this by using those substances to preserve herbs, and you kill two birds with one stone. The basic process is to blend lots of the herb into the carrier, a much higher concentration than normal. Freeze the herb/oil in ice cube trays, the herb/butter in logs or balls, or make extra-strong herbal vinegar (fill a jar with fresh herbs, pour in vinegar to cover, let sit for two weeks). To use, measure out a small amount of the herb concentrate, then add a sufficient measure of plain butter, oil, or vinegar to equal the amount called for in the recipe.

*I*'m going to let you in on a secret: there is no such thing as a houseplant. Think about it: no plant on earth has the inside of your house as its natural home. What we call houseplants are actually outdoor plants that live and thrive in warm climates. Unlike perennials and shrubs that are native to the temperate regions of North America and Europe, they have no in-built need to go through a cold period, and in fact would die if subjected to it. So during our winters, they need to be in a protected environment—inside the house. Just like people.

Most of the plants we use as houseplants are native to the world's tropical regions, and in fact nursery professionals refer to houseplants as "tropicals." A few houseplants come from temperate or semitropical forests, and a few others are native to warm desert regions of the world.

Always keep this in mind, for it is the key to success. The best way to have healthy houseplants is to duplicate, as nearly as is practical, their native conditions. Think jungle, rainforest, desert. Picture what they're like:

- *Jungle*: temperatures are warm year-round, soil is moist, humidity is high, light is bright but filtered by the tall trees.
- *Rainforest:* high humidity, very spongy and lightly damp soil, cooler temperatures, shade with splashes of sunshine.
- *Desert:* high temperatures, bright sun, sandy soil, low humidity.

## *Choosing Houseplants*

The single most important issue with houseplants is their light requirements. In outdoor gardens, even in container gardens on the patio or front stoop, light hits plants from all angles as the sun makes its daily trip across the sky. With houseplants, they get only the light that enters through the window to which they are most closely situated.

How much light comes through that window is a function of whether or not it has curtains and how opaque they are. Of course, the light also depends on which compass direction the window faces.

All other things being equal (same size window, same kind of curtains, no tall buildings in the way):

| | |
|---|---|
| North-facing window | gets the least light. |
| East window | is the next brightest. |
| West window | is brighter still. |
| South window | is brightest of all. |

The smart way to make choices is to decide where in your home you would like to place a houseplant, watch the sun and light patterns there (hold your hand up where the plant will go—how much shadow do you see on a sunny day?), and choose plants that exactly match those conditions.

The normal way it happens is more like this: We go out to buy a plant, lose our heart to some greenhouse beauty, and do the best we can with it once home. More on that shortly.

## How to Pick a Good Houseplant

Whenever you shop for houseplants, follow these guidelines to choose a good supplier and then a good individual plant:

- Look the whole store over. Do you get an overall impression of strong growth and good green color? That could be because they just got in a shipment from the wholesale greenhouse, so by itself this doesn't tell the whole story. But on the other hand if you get a general sense of puny, the plants have probably been neglected. Go somewhere else.

> ## Top 10 Houseplants
>
> These are the toughest of all:
> 1. Chinese evergreen
> 2. Aspidistra (cast-iron plant)
> 3. Spider plant
> 4. Dieffenbachia (dumb cane)
> 5. Dracaena
> 6. Philodendron
> 7. Swedish ivy (aka Creeping Charlie)
> 8. Snake plant
> 9. Spathiphyllum
> 10. Rubber plant

- Are all the leaves extremely shiny, as if they had been waxed? Unless the store has an automatic misting system, the plants have probably been treated with a leaf gloss, which blocks the plant's pores. I'd skip this one.
- Ask for a specific plant by Latin name; see what kind of reaction you get. Again, this doesn't tell you everything but it's a good clue to how knowledgeable the staff is.

Now, pick out one plant that you like, and let's investigate its quality.

- Pick up the pot; if it feels unrealistically lightweight, either it hasn't been watered in a long time (which is not good but also not disastrous) or the roots have completely filled the pot and there is no soil left to retain water. (This is called rootbound, or potbound.) If you suspect the latter, confirm it by the next steps.
- Turn the pot upside down. If you see roots growing out of the drainage hole, pass on this one and get another.
- Look at the top of the soil. If roots are growing there, the plant needed to be transplanted a long time ago. Pass.
- Pull gently upward from the base of the stem.
  1. If the plant comes right up but the soil stays, the plant doesn't have a good root system. Probably somebody chopped off the top of another plant and stuck it in this pot. Pass.
  2. If the plant and the soil and the root ball come up as one unit, and the soil is bone dry, it hasn't been well cared for. Pass.
  3. If the whole thing comes out and the roots are snarled in a thick mass circling around the bottom, that's rootbound. Pass.
- Look closely at the leaves, both top and undersides, at the growing tip, and in

the angles where leaves are attached to the stem. If the plant is infested with insects, this is where the problem will show.

- If you see brown tips on the leaves, or a sharp edge indicating that tips have been trimmed with scissors, the plant has not had the right kind of care and someone has tried to hide the evidence. Pass.
- If you're shopping for a plant that flowers, choose one with more buds than flowers; you'll have a much longer blossom period at home.

## Caring for Your Plant

The very first thing I recommend you do once you get your new baby home is to flush the soil to get rid of the excess amounts of fertilizer it probably received in the shop. Flushing is simple: set the pot in the sink and let *lots* of water run through it.

Next, isolate the new plant for a few days. If it has any insect or disease problems, you don't want to pass them on to your other plants.

Then find the best location, with the most appropriate light. If things are less than ideal in that respect, you can fudge a bit with these techniques:

- Alternate plants: move one high-light plant into a darker corner for a week and switch another plant into its spot.
- Change your curtains to something filmier that lets in more light.
- Place the plants near a mirror, to take advantage of reflected light.
- Install artificial lights (fluorescent or special full-spectrum plant lights) in a special area and rotate plants in and out. (Personally I consider this a last resort.)
- Lower your expectations, and hope for the best. Quite a number of indoor plants will survive in light that is less than ideal. They may not grow perfectly (smaller leaves, for instance) but they will live.

### WATERING

Far more harm is done to plants by overzealous watering than by its opposite. There is no indoor plant that needs watering every day, and hardly any that need watering once a week. In fact, putting yourself on a watering schedule based on the calendar is a mistake: there are too many variables that come into play.

The best approach is to water only when the soil is dry, and the best way to check that is with a tool you always have with you: your finger. Your soil should be nice and loose, and so you should be able to get your finger down a couple of inches. Don't water unless it's dry there. (And if you don't like getting your hands dirty, you don't have much future as a gardener.)

Unless it is too big, take the plant to the water rather than the other way around. Put the plant in the sink and water it until water runs out of the bottom. While it drains, sponge off the leaves and check for signs of insects.

For large plants and hanging baskets, invest in a watering can with a long spout; it's much easier to work with.

Most plants can be watered from the top, but if the leaves are fuzzy (African violets are one common example) water drops can leave spots. The solution is to water from the bottom. Fill the drip tray with water; it will be absorbed up into the soil.

If you already know you tend to be lazy about watering (or if you're gone a lot), you might find it easier to include moisture-retaining polymers in your soil mix; you'll need to water less often. See page 42.

To maintain sensible watering when you're out of town for long periods, you can purchase special pots called "self-watering"; basically, they hold a reservoir of water in a larger than normal drip tray, and an absorbent wick pulls the water up into the soil. You can accomplish the same thing without the additional expense if you rig up either one of the two wicking systems illustrated below.

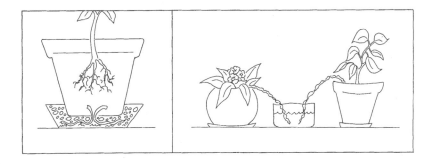

*Two self-wicking systems keep your houseplants watered while you're away. Single pot (left) sits on a tray filled with pebbles and water. One end of a thin strip of absorbent fabric has been threaded up into the drainage hole and the other end lies in the water. On the right, strips torn from an old T-shirt connect several pots to a central reservoir of water.*

The great majority of species we grow as houseplants are native to tropical jungles or semitropical forests, where it is very humid all year long. The need for humidity is an innate part of their nature.

Unfortunately, central heating and air conditioning have done a good job of dehumidifying modern homes. By creating conditions that we humans find comfortable, we have deprived the plants of conditions they would like.

There are some ways to provide a humid mini-climate for the plants:

- *Construct a pebble tray.* Fill a wide, shallow container with small pebbles and add water almost up to top of the pebbles. Set the pot or pots (minus their drip tray) on the pebbles. The water will evaporate into moisture vapor, which will travel straight upward, right to the plants. Replace the water as it evaporates.
- *Use a mister.* Keep a small spray bottle near each plant or group of plants. Whenever you think of it, give them a spritz.
- *Surround the plants with wet moss.* Sphagnum moss holds many times its own weight in water. Get an oversize pot, line the inside with damp moss, and set the plant in its pot down inside. This works better if the plant is in a clay pot, which is porous and can take in moisture through the sides.
- *Put them in humid rooms.* Kitchens are naturally more humid than other rooms in your home, and are a good spot for plants with a high need for humidity. So are bathrooms, provided there is enough light.

Fortunately, most houseplants seem to adapt rather well to humidity levels lower than ideal. Only a few (the ferns, primarily) are really insistent about high humidity.

---

### Houseplants: A Few Surprises

- Any of the cactuses and small succulents look cute on a sunny windowsill and can go for many weeks without watering.
- Bromeliads: a family of plants with many intriguing species, all with fabulous flowers. Buy them in bloom so you know what you're getting. Discard when the flower expires (which will be many months)—it won't bloom again.
- Asparagus fern looks fragile but is actually very tough.
- Unusual succulents include string of hearts (*Ceropegia woodii*), living stones (*Lithops*), both of which look just like what the name suggests, and maternity plant (*Kalanchoe daigremontiana*), which produces itsy little plants all along the edges of the mother plant's leaves.

### FERTILIZING

Outdoors, garden plants pull in nutrients from the soil which, if you are paying attention, you have enriched with lots of organic matter. Indoors, the only replacement source when nutrients are extracted is what we add in the form of fertilizer. (See Fertilizer chapter for general background and specific formulations.)

Houseplants need fertilizing when they are actively growing: spring and summer. In the fall, start tapering off, and withhold entirely in winter. Use a complete fertilizer in a ratio of 2–1–1 for foliage plants, 1–2–1 for plants that flower. Follow the directions on the package for dilution proportions.

*Tip:* When they are vigorously growing (late spring), my houseplants respond very well to a more-but-less fertilizer regimen. I fertilize every time I water with very diluted fertilizer, about 20 percent strength.

### PRUNING

Comparatively speaking, pruning is much less of a problem with houseplants than with outdoor plants. You will need to prune:

- To remove old flower heads on flowering plants.
- When irregular care has produced a plant with a lopsided shape.
- When poor light has produced a plant that is leggy (with long stretches of bare stem between the leaves).
- To remove dead stems or small branches.

Cut off just above a node. Use your fingers if the stems are soft, your garden pruners if not. Scissors don't work well; it's too easy to nick something you didn't intend to.

Houseplants that are botanically vines (they grow in one long line) need a special kind of pruning on a regular basis. It is called "pinching back," because that's what you do: pinch out the growing tip with your fingers (see illustration on page 92). This will cause the plant to branch out horizontally. If you then pinch *those* stems when they grow longer, and continue the process with all new growth, you will have a plant that is full and bushy instead of long and stringy. Among the common houseplants that need pinching back are philodendron, wandering jew, prayer plant, and Swedish ivy.

### CLEANING

In your home, plants collect dust at the same rate as everything else: too fast. It's unsightly, but more important it's unhealthy: it blocks the pores through which

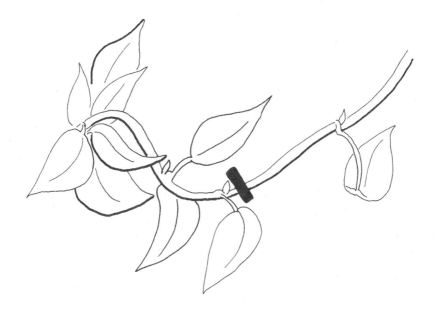

*Houseplants get leggy as they reach for limited light. Prune away the stretched-out stem back to a healthy bud, and put the pot in a better spot with more light.*

the plant transpires, and provides a nice environment for spider mites and other yucky critters.

Here's how to keep them clean:

- If the leaves are flat and broad, wipe them down with a damp cloth or sponge.
- If leaves are fuzzy, brush away the dust with an artist's or a makeup brush, or something equally soft.
- If the plant has lots of tiny leaves, hand wiping would be too tedious. Instead, take it to the sink and rinse it well with the spray attachment. If the plant is too large to fit in the sink, take it outside and rinse it with a soft spray from the garden hose.

## Repotting

After a while, your plant will grow so lustily under your good care that it will need to be moved to a larger pot.

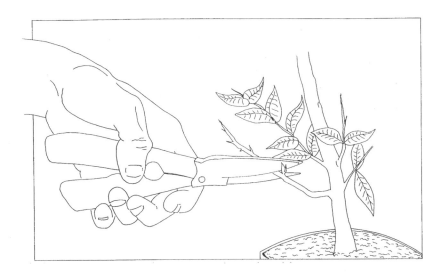

*This damaged stem will not recover. The only sensible thing to do is prune it back.*
*The healthy bud will now develop into a new branch.*

How do you know if it needs repotting? Simple. Take it out of its present pot, following step 4 on page 95, and look at the roots. If they are thickly matted at the bottom, growing around and around in the shape of the pot, it's time. If you see just a few small roots at the edge of the soil ball, or no roots at all, slide everything back into the pot. Check again in six months.

Before we actually begin the repotting itself, we need to get the new pot ready and also the soil that's going in it. So let's take a minute to get acquainted with both.

### POTS

Pots are fabricated from several kinds of material, but for our purposes there are two that are the most important: plastic and clay (also called terra cotta).

- *Plastic pots* are less expensive, less apt to break, and, because they are not porous, hold moisture in the soil better. On the other hand, air doesn't get into the soil as readily. Also, they are not exactly gorgeous.
- *Clay pots* are porous, so air moves into the soil from the sides and water vapor moves out, so they dry out faster. They are heavy, they chip easily, and they're somewhat more expensive.

*The only way to get this single stem to form branches, for an overall bushier shape, is to remove the growing tip. It's called pinching because that's just what you do.*

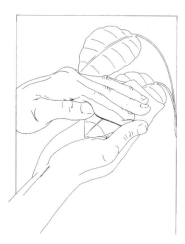

*Keeping houseplants clean and dust-free is the best way to avoid spider mites.
Wipe big leaves with a damp cloth.*

*Gardening from the Ground Up*

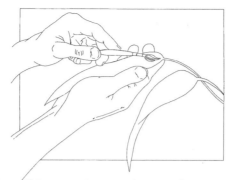

*To get dust off leaves with a very fuzzy surface, use a soft brush.*

If you are growing plants that need frequent watering (ferns, spathiphyllum), you'll probably be happier with plastic pots. Otherwise, the choice is primarily one of personal taste and pocketbook.

---

**The First Law of Pots:**

Don't use anything that doesn't have a drainage hole. Never, ever.

---

Ornamental pots of porcelain, pottery, brass, etc., without drainage holes are intended to be used as outer display containers, with a more pedestrian pot placed inside.

In all cases, be sure to use a saucer under the pot to catch drips.

Pots are measured by their diameter across the top. Usually, but not always, they are that same measure high. A nursery ad for a "6-inch philodendron" refers to a pot of that diameter, not the height of the plant.

When it comes time to repot, move the plant into a pot one size larger than its current container.

### POTTING SOIL

If you are just doing one plant, you may find it simpler to purchase a small bag of houseplant potting mix. But if you have several houseplants (or some outdoor containers too) and the necessary storage space, you will find it more economical in the long run to buy separate bags of the various ingredients and mix your own.

What's in a good houseplant mix?

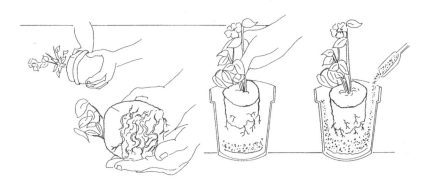

*Repotting a houseplant in three easy steps: (1) Knock the plant out of its current pot, keeping the soil intact. (2) Set it into a pot one size larger that already has some soil in. (3) Fill in the sides with more soil. Water well, to settle the plant, and you're done.*

- **Potting soil.** Sold in garden centers in big bags, so-called potting soil is not really soil, but a mixture of bark chips, bark dust, other ground-up organic matter, some peat moss, and probably a small proportion of perlite (see below). It's okay as is but much better if supplemented with some of the following.
- **A lightener.** In other words, some material to loosen up the particles in the potting soil that would otherwise clump together, and to make the mixture more lightweight.

  Two substances that serve as lighteners are *perlite* and *vermiculite.* Perlite is volcanic rock crushed into very tiny pebbles; it is bright white and weighs practically nothing. Vermiculite is mica broken into tiny bits that are flat and silvery.
- **A moisture-holding conditioner.** Something to improve overall texture and improve the soil's ability to retain moisture. Two good ones are *peat moss* and *sphagnum moss*; actually they are the same material in different forms.

  Sphagnum moss is one of several kinds of mosses, dried and bundled; it looks a bit like a messy bundle of gray-green knitting yarn. Peat moss is sphagnum moss that has been shredded into very fine pieces; it is soft and fluffy, almost like brown talcum powder. Both hold several times their own weight in water.

  All houseplant mixes benefit from some measure of peat or sphagnum moss. If your plant is one that needs very moist soil, add a greater proportion of moss.
- **Sand.** Sand keeps the mixture from compacting, and so makes it drain better.

A little bit is good in any houseplant mix. For cactuses and succulents, add lots of sand; the finished mix should be half sand and half everything else.

## MIXING YOUR OWN SOIL

1. Start with one measure of commercial potting soil.
2. Add in one-half measure of perlite or vermiculite, one-half measure of peat or sphagnum moss, and one quarter measure of sand. (More moss for water lovers, more sand for succulents.)
3. If you wish to use slow-release fertilizer (see page 62) or soil polymers (see page 42), mix them in now.
4. Optional: a pinch of charcoal will help prevent the soil taking on a sour smell over time.

And that's it. Make up a batch and water it very thoroughly. Mix it around with your hands to get the water evenly distributed.

## REPOTTING STEP BY STEP

1. Have your new pot and the extra soil ready. If the new pot is clay, soak it an hour ahead in a bucket of water.
2. Fill the new pot about one-third full with the new soil.
3. Water the plant in its current pot very, very thoroughly; this helps it slide out.
4. Turn the pot upside down, fit one hand around the base of the stem, and knock the edge of the pot against a countertop or table or the heel of your palm. The whole thing should slide out into your hand. If not, run a sharp knife around the inside of the pot to loosen the soil and try again.
5. If the roots are matted together or tightly snarled at the bottom, use your hands to spread them out. Cut off very long ones.
6. Fit the plant and all its existing soil down into the middle of the new pot. Fill in around the edges with new soil, pressing lightly as you go. Leave an inch of head space at the top.
7. Water very thoroughly, to settle the soil and the plant. That's all there is to it.

## WHAT TO DO WITH A VERY LARGE PLANT?

Often people who have a very large indoor plant in a large container have just one container of the right size, and they don't really want the plant to get any bigger. But there comes a time when the plant is so rootbound that it begins to pout, and you have to do something.

The solution is *root pruning*: remove the plant from the container, slice off some of the roots, replace it in the same container, and fill in with new soil.

*To keep a very large plant from becoming rootbound but maintain its size, get a friend to help you slide it from its container and slice off soil and roots around the edges. Reinsert the now-smaller root ball back into the same pot, and fill in with new soil. It is now safe for several more years.*

You probably need someone to help you remove the plant. (If you were really smart and also handy, you could have built a wooden container with one removable side, and then you could do this procedure by yourself.)

Have a large tarp or dropcloth ready, and pull the plant from the container. Then, with a very large and very sharp kitchen knife, slice off sections of the soil ball and the roots. It seems like a barbarous thing to do to a helpless plant, but it actually helps promote new root growth. Besides, if you want to keep the plant to a manageable size, you have no choice.

# Trouble-Shooting: Insects and Human Error

The conditions that houseplants like—warm, humid, moist—are also favored by many damaging insects. Once established, they can prove almost impossible to get rid of. The wiser course is to inspect the plants regularly, say once a month, and take prompt action at the first sign of trouble. If unsuccessful, get rid of the plant; it will only infect the others.

Here's a rogue's gallery of the worst houseplant pests; check the illustrations in the Problems chapter to get a clear picture of the enemy.

**Aphids.** Tiny little bugs, green or black, that clump on top of each other on stems, leaves, or growing tips. They suck the life out of a plant, and just looking at them crawling all over each other gives me the willies. Take the plant outside, if possible, and spray it with a weak solution of dishwashing detergent in water. Spray again, hard, to rinse the leaves and remove the insects. Keep checking for several weeks, and repeat if necessary.

**Mealybugs.** Very small insects covered over with a cottony material that looks like the end of a cotton swab. They cluster on the stems right at the leaf joints. Paint them with a cotton swab dipped in alcohol. However, a heavy infestation is almost impossible to get rid of. You're better off tossing the plant.

**Spider mites,** also called red spiders. They actually are spiders and they are red, but they're so minute you can't really see them. What you see instead is their webs, on the leaves or the joints where the leaf attaches to the stem. Wipe away the webs whenever you see them. Best of all, prevent the mites in the first place by keeping the plant free of dust and keeping the humidity high.

**Scale.** These are small insects with hard brown shells, usually found on the stems of plants. Use an old toothbrush to scrape them off, and pick up the bodies that fall onto the soil. Wash stems with soapy water.

You might have noticed I didn't say anything about spraying infected plants with insecticides. Frankly, I don't feel comfortable using toxic materials inside the house. The methods described above will work most of the time. If not, give the plant a decent burial and buy another. Life goes on.

| *If Your Plant Shows* | *Your Problem Is Probably* |
|---|---|
| Brown leaf tips | Not enough humidity; too much fertilizer; improper watering. |
| Small leaves, weak growth | Not enough light; needs fertilizer; needs repotting. |
| Pale leaves | Not enough light. |
| Dry, withered leaves | Humidity too low. |
| Yellow leaves at bottom | Too much watering. |
| Yellow leaves with green veins | Needs iron. |
| Bottom leaves dropping | Overwatering. |
| Brown circles on leaves | Burned by direct sun. |
| Mildew | Too much humidity or water. Remove damaged leaves; use fungicide if severe. |

**M**any people who are new to gardening are thoroughly intimidated by the scientific names of plants. I hope to ease your anxiety a little bit.

It helps if you understand the rationale behind the naming. Every single plant in the world has one, and only one, scientific name. So if people use that name when referring to the plant, there is never any confusion about which they mean. Common names, on the other hand, range all over the place; any one plant can have several different common names in different parts of the world. You can imagine the potential for confusion.

The name itself has two parts. The first part, always capitalized, is the name of the genus to which that plant belongs; the second part is the species. A genus (pronounced *jean*-us) contains several species. For example:

*Pinus strobus*

*Pinus* is the genus to which all pines belong; *Pinus strobus* is the species known as white pine. It's rather like people's names, when they are presented surname first: Twain, Mark. To refer to a plant, you need both names; you wouldn't say just *strobus*, for by itself it has no meaning.

When two plants of the same genus are mentioned close together, the genus name is abbreviated after the first mention, like this:

*Pinus strobus*
*P. contorta* (shore pine)

If that were all there was to it, scientific names would be fairly simple. But in the world of plants, especially cultivated garden plants, there are subcategories and sometimes sub-subcategories within species, known as subspecies, varieties, and cultivars. Often there is a distinct difference between two varieties of the same species, and the point of difference might be just the feature you are looking for. Let's continue with the white pine example.

*Pinus strobus* 'Nana' is a dwarf form. Whereas the regular species gets 100 feet tall, 'Nana' stays around 3 or 4 feet. If you accidentally put the species tree in a rock garden, you'd be in for a nasty surprise in about five years.

# *Latin 101*

Think of this as learning a new language, which of course it is. And take heart—you already know quite a few Latin names: rhododendron, camellia, philodendron, begonia, daphne, sequoia, zinnia, etc. Start adding to your vocabulary one word at a time.

You'll soon realize that some of the same basic words tend to turn up over and over. Also, since Latin is the root of so many English words, you'll be able to figure out many scientific names by looking for familiar words or prefixes. You may notice minor spelling differences, for in Latin, as in many Romance languages, adjectives change their endings to match the nouns. Thus we have *Pelargonium tomentosum* (hairy-leafed geranium) and *Tilia tomentosa* (hairy linden tree). Just focus on the main part of the word, and look for recognizable English derivatives.

| | |
|---|---|
| phyllum | leaf |
| folium | leaf |
| dendron | tree |
| flora | flower |
| macrophyllum | big-leaf |
| floribunda | many-flowered |
| angustifolium | narrow-leaf |
| latifolia | broad-leaf |
| grandiflora | large flowered |
| heterophylla | has different leaves |
| undulatus | wavy-edged (leaves) |
| lanceolatum | lance-shaped (leaves) |
| contortum | twisted |
| odoratum | fragrant |
| repens | creeping |
| recumbens | low-growing |
| prostratum | prostrate (growth habit) |
| palmatum | with large lobes, like a hand |
| tomentosum | hairy, fuzzy |

In addition to terms like these that describe some characteristic of the plant, some Latin names honor a person (perhaps the person who first identified it) or the part of the world where the species grows. Words you can't immediately decipher may well be either of those groups. For instance: *rothschildiana* (the Baron Rothschild), *biebersteinii* (von Bieberstein, German botanist), *skinneri* (George Skinner, orchid collector). And *chinensis* (from China), *japonica* (Japan), *brasiliensis* (Brazil).

Untangling the meaning is sort of fun, once you get the hang of it. But figuring out the pronunciation can be tricky. Most of the time, you will encounter the name in print, in a book or catalog, and won't have to say it out loud. Otherwise, approach this as you would any other foreign language: keep your ears open whenever you're around someone who speaks it, and copy what they do. In addition, some reference books include helpful pronunciation guides.

In this book, I have used a hybrid approach. In general text, where an individual species is not relevant, common names are used. I also used common names where there is no possibility of confusion: if I say lilac, you wouldn't be likely to picture a lily.

**LAWNS**

What with mowing, watering, fertilizing, aerating, and thatching, a lawn requires more regular maintenance than any other element in a garden. To cut down on all that labor, and also to conserve water, an increasingly precious resource in much of the country, many homeowners are using ground covers instead.

Still, there is nothing like a beautiful expanse of lush green grass to set off your accent trees and flower beds. And you just can't get a good game of croquet going on a ground cover. Besides, chances are you inherited a lawn when you bought your house, and now you need to know how to take care of it.

## Getting Acquainted with the Grasses

The first thing to know about lawn grasses is that they are not all the same. All the many different species of grass used in lawns can be grouped into two basic types: warm-season and cool-season. Cool-season grasses have their primary growth period in the spring, with a lesser spurt in fall; in hot weather, they don't do much. Because they withstand cold weather well, they are used in northern areas. Warm-season grasses flourish in summer and go dormant in colder months, turning a golden brown. They are used in warmer areas of the country, where summer heat would destroy the cool-season grasses.

So, if you live in the South and your lawn goes brown in winter, it's not because you did anything wrong. If you don't like the look, you can overseed with a cool-season variety, and have green grass year-round (along with year-round mowing). In northern climates, your cool-season grass will stay rich and green through the summer only if you water it aggressively.

The most common grass varieties are listed here. However, most grass seed, while it may be all warm-season types or all cool-season, is a mix of several varieties. Seldom is a lawn planted with just one species; there is too much chance of losing the entire lawn to a disease or unusual weather conditions. Also, with a mixture you get a longer period of green; when one species is fading at the end of its natural season of growth, another in the mixture is at its prime.

If you are in the position of putting in a new lawn, or buying seed to fill in bare spots in the existing lawn, the following tables will help you understand the contents of the package you are looking at. Most of the time, you can expect that what is offered for sale in a good garden center will be appropriate for your area. If you feel the need for more information, consult the experts at your County Extension office.

### COOL-SEASON GRASSES

| species | comments |
|---|---|
| Colonial bent grass; creeping bent grass | Used for golf courses; tolerate partial shade. |
| Kentucky bluegrass | Most popular cool-season grass. |
| Tall, hard, and creeping red fescue | Tolerate shade well; usually mixed with other species. |
| Annual and perennial ryegrass | Grow fast; used to overseed warm-season grasses. |

### WARM-SEASON GRASSES

| species | comments |
|---|---|
| Bermuda grass | Handles foot traffic well. Great for play areas. |
| St. Augustine grass | Tolerates heat, shade, and heavy wear. |
| Zoysia | Tolerates heat and drought; good choice for play areas. |

### GRASSES FOR YOUR AREA OF THE COUNTRY

| | |
|---|---|
| Northeast | Colonial and creeping bent grass; bluegrass; ryegrass. |
| Southeast | Bermuda grass, tall fescue, zoysia; bluegrass and ryegrass in cooler transitional climates, St. Augustine in warmer zones. |
| Tropical South | Bermuda, St. Augustine, and zoysia; overseeded with bent grass, fescues, or ryegrass. |
| Mountains, Plains | Fescues and bluegrass; but native grasses are best choice. |
| Southwest | Bermuda, zoysia, St. Augustine; overseeded with ryegrass. |
| West Coast | Bent grass, bluegrass, fescues, ryegrass. |

*A beautiful lawn begins with a very smooth surface. This tool, a leveler, can be rented at tool rental shops. If you're handy you can build your own; if you use wood, lash something heavy securely to the top, to provide the necessary weight.*

A third category is the native grasses, the species that, in contrast to the usual lawn grasses, grow wild in certain areas of the country. Native grasses are extremely tough, resistant to drought and disease, and, because they are usually left to grow in their normal way, require little maintenance. They do not produce the smooth, formal-looking surface we usually associate with lawns, but they have their own beauty. They are gaining in popularity in prairie and desert areas of the West, where water conservation is a major goal.

The best-known natives are buffalo grass, native to the prairie; beach grass, which grows as well in sandy desert as on its native beaches; and crested wheatgrass, in mountains and high-desert regions. (Ornamental grasses, a different kettle of fish, are briefly described in the chapter on Perennials.)

# Putting in a New Lawn

Starting from scratch, with a totally bare palette, you have primarily two choices: plant seed or lay sod. Sod is the name given to "ready-to-go" strips. Commercial turf farms grow huge fields of grass, which they dig up in long strips, roots and all, ready to be laid on prepared soil; it's not unlike buying squares of carpet. (A few types of grass, primarily warm-season varieties, are planted in what are called plugs or sprigs: individual small plants.)

In either case, it is extremely important that your soil is in good condition. Review the chapter on Soil; if you have heavy clay soil, poor drainage, or nutrient-poor soil, now is the time to fix those problems—not after your new lawn is growing, or trying to. Even if the soil is basically of good quality, adding in organic matter will help get the grass off to a strong start, and the process of adding it will serve to loosen and lighten the soil. Also, if you intend to install an automatic watering system, now is the time to do it.

After you have worked in the necessary soil amendments, the next step is to smooth the surface, using a tool called a leveler. If you wish to add a brick or concrete edging strip, to make mowing easier, do it at this point.

*Seed* is best applied with a mechanical spreader of some kind; you get much more even coverage than you can accomplish by hand. The two examples shown here are among the most common kinds of spreaders; they can also be used to spread granular fertilizer evenly, which is your next step. Rake the entire area, to lightly "bury" the seed.

The best time to sow grass seed is in the spring; second best is fall. If you can expect plentiful rain during those periods, you can stop here. But if spring is hot and dry where you live, cover the seed with a mulch, like peat moss, that you have already soaked in water.

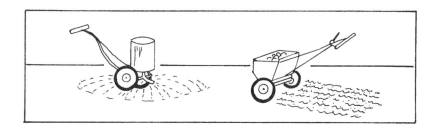

*Mechanical spreaders spray grass seed (and dry fertilizer) in a circular pattern (left) or in wide rows. Both give more even coverage than you can do by hand.*

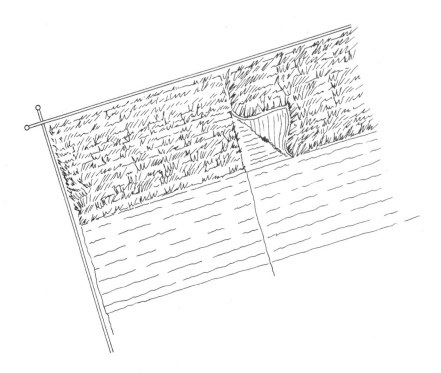

*Laying sod strips gives you an instant lawn. Prepare the soil surface underneath just as thoroughly as if you were going to seed, then fit the lawn strips end to end, as if you were laying carpet tiles. Water well for several weeks, until the roots grow through into your soil.*

Keep the area damp until grass is germinated. Pay attention; you may need to do this every day if the weather is warm. Most grass seed germinates in two to three weeks.

*Sod* can be laid any time of the year. What you get is instant lawn; what you give up to get it is a lot more money.

With sod as with seed, you must start with loose, rich soil in good condition; it should be lightly damp. Lay the sod pieces end to end, with no overlaps. Use a strong knife to cut around edging strips or similar obstructions. From a rental center, rent a lawn roller, which looks like a large barrel lying sideways, with a handle like a lawnmower. Fill it half full with water and roll the entire area, to make sure the roots are in good contact with the soil. Keep the sod well watered during the first six weeks, mow when necessary, and you're done.

Ripping out old lawn, amending and grading the soil, and putting in new sod or seed is such a horrendous job you might prefer to call in a professional.

# Maintaining a Lawn

Whether you planted it or inherited it, your lawn will be beautiful and lush only if you make the commitment to take care of it.

### WATERING

Most people water their lawn too much. Your goal should be to water only when the soil is dry 2 inches down, rather than by the calendar. Of course it will become dry faster in warm weather, so you will have to check periodically until you learn to "read" your grass. Take something like a screwdriver or a long weeding tool, stick it down into the grass and pull it aside until you have opened up a space you can get your finger down into. If it's dry, water; if not, wait. Another test: walk on the grass. If your footprints remain, your lawn needs water.

The chapter on Water shows several different types of sprinklers. Any of them works fine with lawns; just be sure to move them around to get full coverage.

The general rule is, your lawn needs water most at the time it is actively growing, which is spring for cool-season grasses and summer for warm-season types. As with everything else, deep watering less often is better than shallow watering frequently.

### FERTILIZING

Usually you add fertilizer to an existing lawn once or twice in the spring, and perhaps again in the early fall. The formula should be high in nitrogen (see chapter on Fertilizer).

The physical form of fertilizer—powder, granules, liquid—is a matter of your own convenience. Just realize that dry fertilizer begins to work only when it becomes moist, so water thoroughly once you're done.

More important than what you use is that you apply it evenly. Mechanical spreaders like the one you may have used to spread grass seed do an excellent job of applying fertilizer evenly, and so they are commonly used with lawns.

A special category of fertilizer is generically called "weed-and-feed." It contains both fertilizer for the lawn and an herbicide for broadleaf weeds. Follow directions on the package for application rate.

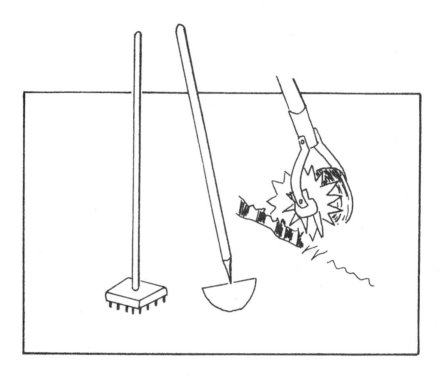

*Simple hand tools for important lawn tasks. Aerator (left) opens up holes in thick lawn so air and water can penetrate; step down on the flat surface. Edging tool (center) slices cleanly when you step on it like a shovel. Rolling edger (right) rolls along sidewalks or edging strips, and the rotating wheel trims grass to a neat edge.*

### DETHATCHING

When you mow your lawn, the cut pieces fall down and accumulate at the base of the grass stems; that accumulation is thatch. A little bit of thatch is good, for the grass clippings, when they decompose, put nitrogen back into the soil. But a thick buildup of thatch will block water from getting to the roots of the lawn, and so it must be removed.

Grasp a section of lawn with your hand, pulling back the grass to expose the thatch layer; it's brown or yellow and obviously dead. Now poke your finger through to the soil. If the thatch is more than half an inch thick, it needs to be removed.

It is possible to do this by hand, using a heavy rake to pull out the thatch, but it is a miserable job. You can rent a special machine called a dethatcher that cuts down through thatch vertically and lifts up chunks. Make a complete pass in one direction and go over the area again at right angles.

## AERATING

Aerating is not the same as thatching. It means opening up small holes in the soil to allow air to move into soil that has become very compacted from people walking on the lawn. You probably need to do this once a year, twice if you have clay soil.

You can rent an aerating machine that runs over the area like a lawnmower, or use a mechanical device with lots of spikes that you step down on, like a shovel (see illustration on page 108). Or you can strap special aerators onto your shoes and walk around the lawn.

And then of course there is . . .

## MOWING

Speaking very generally, most grass should be kept at a height of 1 to 2 inches. If you don't wait too long between mowings, you can safely let the clippings fall to the ground; they will be so small they will disintegrate quickly, and you'll have minimum thatch buildup.

Whether you use a push mower or a gas- or electric-powered model is purely a matter of choice. The gentle whir of a push mower has it all over the power types in noise and general esthetics, and they work fine as long as your lawn is not gargantuan or very hilly. Just be sure to have them sharpened each year.

Don't always mow in the same direction. Alternate your pattern, so as not to develop ruts in the soil or obvious lines in the grass.

Hand in hand with mowing goes edging—trimming away the grass that grows over the edge of the lawn area into whatever lies beyond: the flower bed, the patio, or the sidewalk. You can do this manually with an edger, a step-on tool with a flat surface and a rounded cutting edge (see illustration on previous page), or a power edging tool. The choice has largely to do with how young your legs are.

One final note: winter care of lawns is generally easy, since they don't need mowing and shouldn't be watered or fertilized. But try not to walk on grass when it is frozen; it is easily damaged in that brittle state.

*T*hey start arriving in the January gloom, just when you're fed up with cold weather and longing to see something green. You snuggle up on the couch with one of them and a cup of tea, and spend blissful hours dreaming over the pictures and the promise of spring.

Mail-order catalogs make a gardener's heart sing as few other things can. Once you order from one, or subscribe to a gardening magazine, or fill out a card at a gardening show, you'll find yourself inundated.

Never turn them down, never throw them away. These catalogs are the best and cheapest way I know of to learn what plants look like, and they are a tremendous resource for planning your next garden area (see the cut-and-paste technique described in the chapter on Design).

But what's it like to actually order from a catalog? What do you get, and how can you be assured of good quality?

## *Finding the Catalogs*

To get you started, I have included in the back of this book a highly opinionated listing of catalogs. I concentrated on companies that provide good information along with the pretty pictures; all of them are reliable, honest, and work very hard to provide good products. I have a personal bias toward small, family-run businesses, but this is not to say the big-daddy firms don't do a good job, because they do.

The catalogs listed in this book represent only the tip of the iceberg. There are hundreds, maybe thousands, of others. To find them:

- Check the "Plant and Seed Sources" section of *Gardening By Mail* (see Bookshelf in the Appendix of this book).
- Browse through several gardening magazines in the library. Take along a notepad and jot down addresses from the ads.

*Your package from a mail-order nursery may contain potted plants, several bareroot plants, and seeds.*

# Ordering Plants and Seeds by Mail

Truth to tell, I myself have never had a bad experience with mail-order nurseries, and I don't know of anyone who has. Common sense tells me it's bound to happen occasionally, but my own very unscientific sample tells me this is a high-quality industry.

However, you will want to be a smart consumer:

- Compare prices of the same item from several catalogs.
- Order a few items from several sources and compare their service.
- Check whatever the company has to say about its guarantee; often this comes in the form of a friendly letter from the owner, up near the front of the catalog.

The tricky part about ordering garden materials is not quality, it's discipline—the discipline to keep your order within reason; you will be sorely tempted to get one of everything. If you order seeds, you also need the discipline to wait until the proper planting time.

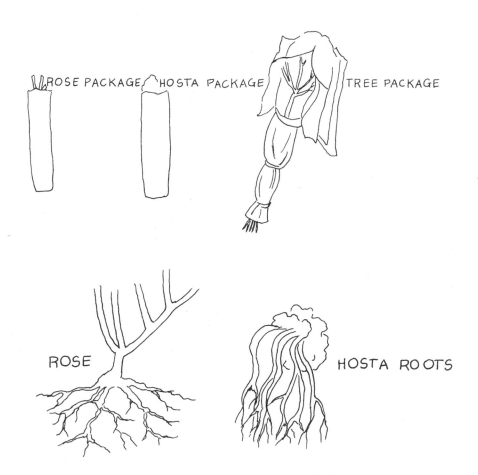

ROSE PACKAGE    HOSTA PACKAGE    TREE PACKAGE

ROSE    HOSTA ROOTS

*Mail-order bareroot plants are packaged very tightly in moisture-retaining material, so the roots don't dry out in transit. Open the packages immediately. You'll see that indeed there is a live plant inside.*

## What You Get, and What to Do with It

- Seeds come in the familiar packets; on the back of the packet is information about when to plant them and where, either directly in the ground or indoors first (see Seeds chapter). Set the packets aside until that time comes.
- Some small plants (perennial herbs, for example) come in small pots. Remove the packing material, and start the process of hardening off the baby plant (see page 184).

- Bulbs come in bags, boxes, or other packages. Open up the package to allow air circulation. If it's not time to plant them (see Bulbs chapter), store them in a dark, cool spot like the basement or garage.
- Most live plants—perennials, roses, young trees—are shipped in a condition called "bareroot." It means just what it sounds like: the roots are bare, not growing in a container or any kind of soil. To keep them from drying out, the roots are encased in some kind of moisture-holding medium like sphagnum moss and the whole thing is wrapped tightly in plastic.

A packed bareroot plant looks weird. The first time you open a box from a mail-order shipment, you may think you got a dud. Even after you remove the packing material and spread out the roots, you may think the plant is dead because you don't see any green parts. But trust me, that's what it's supposed to look like.

What you *do* have to be concerned about is the condition of the roots. Pull aside the moss and look; they should be firm and plump, not completely dry and shriveled. If they are, return the plant and ask for a replacement.

Most mail-order operations schedule their shipments so that live plants arrive at your doorstep at about the right time for planting. If you're ready to plant—if the weather is right and your ground is prepared—unwrap the plant and soak the roots in water. Otherwise, you can put plants in a kind of holding pattern using a technique called heeling in. (See pages 131 and 132.)

See Planting chapter for step-by-step instructions.

**MULCH**

*M*ulch is one of those words you hear a lot once you start hanging around with gardeners. For good reason: it's important, it's relatively easy, and it produces wonderful results.

At its simplest, mulch is any material that lies on top of the soil around plants. It serves three important purposes:

1. It holds moisture in the soil, especially valuable in arid areas or in the dead of summer.
2. It dramatically cuts down on the weed population. And even if some weeds do make it up through the mulch, they're a lot easier to pull up.
3. It provides a blanket of insulation, keeping the plant's base and roots warmer in very cold weather and cooler in very hot weather.

And, depending on what you use for your mulch, it can also contribute an attractive texture and a finished look to your garden.

---

*Easy Garden Tip*

Weeding gets old in a hurry. Smart solution: don't let them get started in the first place. Cover all bare soil with mulch, and weeds have no foothold.

---

## Organic Mulches

Mulches made from organic material are generally pleasing to look at, are easy to shape and position around the plants, and gradually break down into smaller and smaller particles, with the eventual result that they improve soil texture. The flip side of that particular coin is, they must be renewed every year or so.

The most common organic mulches are:

• Bark chips or bark dust, available in large bags at garden

*Several inches of mulch around this young tree holds moisture in the soil and cut down on weeds. Leave a bit of air space right around the trunk.*

centers or by the truckload from garden supply businesses or companies that cut logs into firewood. They are what you would think: ground-up tree bark, in two sizes (chips are larger).

- Pine needles, available free from anyone who has pine trees growing in their yards.
- Hay or straw, available in bales at large farm supply stores.

A little ingenuity will turn up other, often free sources of mulch:

- Dried leaves raked up from the lawn.
- Grass clippings (but spread them out to dry first; a pile of wet clippings turns stinky real fast).
- Tree chips from a tree trimmer; if you're not too far out of their way, they will often give you the chips to save themselves the landfill fee.

Because organic mulches do pack down in winter rains and disintegrate over time, pile them high around vulnerable plants; 12 inches is not too much. Leave a little breathing room between the mulch and the stems and trunks of your plants.

## Inorganic Mulches

Mulches made from inorganic materials do not break down—which is either good or bad, depending on what you use. Common inorganic mulches include:

- Black plastic or landscape cloth. Ugly, but effective.
- Gravel. Ditto. Needs a new layer every few years, because the individual rocks work themselves down into the soil.
- Crushed rock. Similar to gravel but larger pieces. Can look either tacky or zen-like, depending on the skill of the applicator and the eye of the beholder.
- River rock. Larger stones from a river bottom, polished smooth by the river's motion. Creates a starkly beautiful landscape.
- Oyster shells. Yes, I know they are technically organic, but whole shells spread as a mulch will last your lifetime. If you're lucky enough to live near one, ask your favorite oyster bar or cannery to give you the empty shells.

## The Pros and Cons of Plastic

Black plastic is sold in hardware stores, garden centers, and variety stores, usually in rolls 25 feet long and 10 feet wide, and in several thicknesses. It is inexpensive and does its job well. It is not pretty, and it does not usually last beyond one year. If you ever want to till that area, you'll have to remove the plastic first (organic mulches can just be tilled under). And if you snag one end of it with your lawnmower, you have a mess. If your household is dedicated to an environmentally friendly lifestyle, you probably will opt for some organic mulch material.

A relatively new variant is a material known as landscape cloth or landscape fabric. It's similar to black plastic except considerably thicker, so it stays in place better and lasts several years. It is also permeable, so air and water can get through to the soil beneath. As you might imagine, it is considerably more expensive than plain black plastic.

Black plastic is especially valuable for large areas where you're putting in a new ground cover and in vegetable gardens. In the first case, it keeps grass and weeds from sprouting while the ground cover is getting established. You'll probably want to add a layer of bark dust to hide the plastic. (See chapter on Ground Covers for more on the plastic debate.)

In vegetable beds, plastic not only reduces the need for watering and blocks out weeds, it has one other very important benefit: it warms up the soil so you can get a jump on planting warm-season vegetables like tomatoes and peppers.

By the way, you can also buy clear plastic, and it is often on the shelves next to the black. Clear plastic is great for shaping a temporary weather protection around plants and as a mulch it does hold in moisture. But it does absolutely nothing to block weeds; in fact, because it warms the soil and lets in sunlight, it encourages them.

Because mulches are so effective at holding in moisture, they create a breeding ground for slugs and snails, which thrive in damp, cool conditions.

If slugs are a problem where you live, you'll have to balance your need for mulch against your disgust of these pests. It's one of the gardener's most difficult trade-offs.

*T*hese two terms are closely intertwined.

*Native plants* are those that grow naturally in a particular area—in other words, what you would find growing wild. The area in question may be as small as one region of one state, or a large ecological unit encompassing several states, but always where the geography is similar: elevation, topography, climate patterns, type of soil, and so forth, all the conditions that make an area friendly for some plants and inhospitable for others. Thus we say that certain plants are native to the Plains states, to southern California, to the maritime Northwest, to the mountains of western North Carolina, to coastal New England, to the Colorado Plateau in the Southwest—wherever a defined set of conditions exists.

The term *native* has a precise meaning for botanists, but most gardeners tend to use the word casually, meaning "what grows in the woods around here." However, take note: do *not* go out in the woods and dig these plants up, and do not get them from anyone who did. Buy only nursery stock, propagated by responsible greenhouses.

How do you know what plants are native to your area?

- Visit a large nursery or garden center; many set aside a portion of the display area for native plants.
- Watch for local classes or lectures sponsored by garden clubs, parks departments, botanical gardens, arboretums, hiking clubs, environmental groups, etc. They may be titled something like "Wildflowers of the Ozarks."

## Why Native Plants?

Gardeners enjoy growing native plants for reasons that are practical, esthetic, and philosophical.

Other things being equal, native plants will do better in home gardens than "exotic" landscape plants. The reasoning is simple: If you concentrate on plants that are native to your area, then you probably already have the right conditions for growing them and do not have to go to extraordinary lengths to change the soil, install drainage remedies, and so on.

Another related reason that appeals to people with an interest in protecting the environment is that native plants require less fertilizer and less pesticides, insecticides, fungicides, herbicides, and all the other "ides" that they would like to stay away from.

Some people enjoy growing native plants purely for esthetic reasons—they like the look and have chosen it as a theme for their garden. Perhaps they enjoy hiking in the forest or meadow and want to re-create that sensibility in their home garden. And that brings us to natural gardening.

## Natural Gardens

The natural garden is one that echoes, either to some literal degree or in feeling, a natural landscape. It is carefully planned and constructed to look as if Mother Nature planted it. There are no plants in rows, no straight lines, no symmetrical positioning, no apparent patterns. Instead, there is a free-form, free-flowing mix of sizes, shapes, textures. It looks random, but it is not accidental.

Nor is it messy. Natural gardens require the same thoughtful care as any other kind: they need watering if rainfall is inadequate, fertilizing now and then, and regular pruning, dividing, and general tidying up.

A coherent, cohesive natural garden will stick with just one type of landscape—alpine meadow, low-elevation woodland, prairie, high desert plateau, seashore—ideally, one that is geographically compatible to your home. You could, I suppose, force a rain forest type of garden in your Iowa backyard, but it would look a bit strange.

**ORGANIC GARDENING**

*M*ore confusion persists on the question of what *organic* means than perhaps any other term in gardening.

At its most basic, the word refers to something that is, or once was, alive. In the garden, it means substances that are made from plant or animal sources, rather than synthetic chemicals. Thus, when organic gardeners use commercial fertilizers and pesticides, they use only organic versions of those products.

Strictly speaking, organic does not mean the same thing as nonpoisonous. There are some organic garden products that are highly toxic. But because people who prefer organic products usually do so out of strongly held health and environmental concerns, they tend to favor other natural, environmentally sensitive practices in the garden and in all other aspects of their lives.

So, in this broader sense, organic gardening has come to include the following practices:

- *Making and using compost.* Decomposed plant materials are both an excellent all-around soil conditioner, and a way to recycle garden and kitchen waste products. See Compost chapter for how to make and apply it.
- *Controlling insects and pests with natural, nontoxic methods.* Picking harmful insects off plants by hand, introducing into the garden their natural predators, and brewing up homemade, nonsynthetic sprays are standard practices of organic gardeners. Insecticides kill beneficial insects and soil bacteria along with the harmful insects.
- *Focus on prevention.* When the garden area is kept clean, with a minimum of weeds, dead leaves, and other debris, insects have fewer places to breed. And they find it harder to take hold in a garden full of healthy, vigorous plants.
- *Using tried-and-true garden methods and common sense.* Two old-fashioned techniques that still work for vegetable gardeners are crop rotation and companion planting. In the first, plants that are vulnerable to infestation of insects that live over the winter in the ground are planted in a different spot next year. In the second case, plants that seem to have a beneficial effect on other plants are planted together.
- *Viewing the garden as a natural ecosystem,* with good and bad elements. Those who garden organically consider the insects part of the overall picture; they try to maintain a reasonable perspective about how much damage the bugs

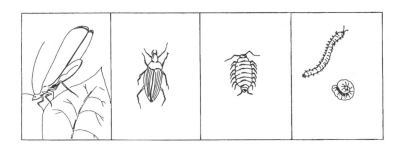

*Four good guys; when you see them in the garden, say thank you and leave them in peace. Left to right: Lacewings eat aphids, scale, and caterpillars. Ground beetles eat slug eggs, cutworms, and root maggots. Sow bugs eat decaying organic matter, helping the process; they roll into a tight ball when disturbed. Millipedes also help break down organic matter in soil.*

do compared to how much damage poisons do to the world. They tend to place little value on picture-perfect tomatoes.

- *Using poisons as a last resort.* Serious problems require serious treatment; organic gardeners use pesticides when the situation calls for it, but only after they have tried other, nontoxic approaches. Even then, they try to find the least harmful control that will still do the job.

### Organic Controls for the Bad Guys

Here are a few of my favorite homemade remedies for the pests and diseases that really damage plants:

- *Aphids.* Dissolve 1 tablespoon cayenne (from your spice shelf) in a pint of hot water; squirt directly onto the little devils.
- *Aphids.* Make up a weak solution of dishwashing detergent or liquid soap in water (about 1 tablespoon to a quart of water) and spray on all nearby plants. Aphids don't like being on the soapy surface.
- *Aphids, scale, mealybugs, spider mites.* Here is a homemade version of horticultural oils, which work by smothering insects and their eggs. Mix 1/2 cup vegetable oil with 1 teaspoon liquid detergent. Dilute it in water (1 tablespoon of the mixture in 1 cup water) and spray all over leaves and stems.
- *Slugs.* Mix one part ammonia (or chlorine bleach) with two parts water. Put it in a spray bottle or a squirt gun and carry it around in your pocket while you're in the garden. Shoot to kill.
- *Powdery mildew.* Dissolve 2 teaspoons baking soda (which is alkaline) and 1/2 teaspoon dishwashing detergent (to help the solution adhere) in a gallon of water. Spray all over leaves at first sign of trouble.
- *Scale.* Scrub off with an old toothbrush and soapy water.

The dictionary definition of *perennial* implies that it's something that goes on forever. In the garden, this is not literally true. Certain plants are called perennial to distinguish them from annuals, which live their whole lives in one year, or biennials, which live two years (see Annuals chapter). It doesn't mean they live forever, just that they live longer than two years. Some start to peter out after four or five years; others live ten, fifteen, even twenty years.

In a pure dictionary sense, trees and shrubs could be considered perennials. But the term has a narrower definition for gardeners. Generally speaking, it refers to plants whose foliage dies completely to the ground in winter but reappears again in the spring. Also speaking generally, when we talk about perennials we expect to see some flowers. There are exceptions to those two, but what *always* sets a perennial apart from a shrub is that shrubs have tough, hard stems like tree branches (the gardeners' term is *woody*) and perennials do not. That is also why roses are not considered perennials, even though they live longer than two years.

A special group of perennials are those plants that build a thick underground storage system to carry them through the winter—bulbs and their cousins. Because so many gardeners assign them a different spot in their minds, separate from perennials, we assign them their own spot in this book.

## Choosing Perennials

A person can easily get dizzy thinking about perennials. They represent a wider range of plants than any other category of green things, with different sizes, shapes, colors, textures, flower shapes, and growth habits.

To make good choices, start by reflecting on your ideal garden and review some of the principles in the chapter on Design. What colors do you like? Are you trying to achieve a certain look or mood? Do you want the longest possible period of bloom? And so forth. Then, do all you can to learn what the various plants look like and behave like. Spend *lots* of time looking at catalogs and at other people's gardens.

---

### Top 10 Perennials for Shade

1. Primroses. There are several nice varieties suitable for woodland settings.
2. Foxglove. Tall and dramatic. Native foxgloves are biennial, but new hybrid varieties are true perennials.
3. Fuchsia. There are several hardy varieties that will regrow from roots if cold temperatures kill the above-ground foliage.
4. Virginia bluebells. Short-lived plant, but worth growing (and replacing).
5. Violets. Some are evergreen, some die back in winter. Wonderful range of flower color—white, pink, yellow, rose, and of course violet; some have richly colored leaves as well. Most are wonderfully fragrant and bloom early, even in winter.
6. Trillium. A beautiful woodland native plant; blooms early spring. Buy only plants that were propagated in a nursery, not collected in the wild.
7. Bleeding heart. An old-fashioned plant that still enchants with its unusual flower. The native species has ferny foliage and spreads like crazy. The domesticated hybrid, noninvasive, is a better choice.
8. Pulmonaria. Known as Bethlehem sage, Jerusalem cowslip, and lungwort. Sassy spotted leaves and tiny pink, white, blue, or purple flowers.
9. Columbine. Fairyland flowers in a wonderful range of colors hang upside down. Many varieties have bicolor flowers. An old-fashioned charmer.
10. Hellebores. Mostly evergreen plants with flowers in winter and early spring. Two popular varieties are Lenten rose and Christmas rose.

---

### Top 10 Perennials for Sun

1. Yarrow
2. Artemisia
3. Veronica
4. Aster
5. Coreopsis
6. Oriental poppy
7. Purple cone flower (*Echinacea*)
8. Peony
9. Baby's breath
10. Daylily

# Designing a Perennial Border

Perennial borders are very popular these days; you'll see many articles about them in the gardening magazines. But you might not be clear as to what a "perennial border" is. That's because the term has come to be used rather loosely.

Basically, it means any garden plot that is longer than it is wide and has at least one side that is contiguous with some architectural element: your property line, the side of the house, the side of the garage, a fence, a sidewalk, or a path or walkway. About the only one that doesn't qualify is a flower plot surrounded on all sides by lawn or ground cover; those are referred to as "island beds." A "mixed border" is one that has other types of plants in addition to perennials: annuals, bulbs, shrubs, maybe even a small tree or two.

In either case, when it comes to designing a perennial or mixed border, you have to see the border as an entity unto itself and also as an element in the larger garden. The only time you can get away with incompatible border styles is if the ones that clash can never be viewed at the same time from any normal vantage point.

The perimeters of the border can be, but do not have to be, straight lines. If you have a border along a fence, obviously one perimeter is defined by the fence line. But the shape of the other three sides is up to you. Using curved lines adds movement and rhythm to your design.

Many gardeners use beds and borders as individual paintings, experimenting with colors and shapes. A border, because it is a discrete unit, is the perfect place to try different plants and combinations. Just keep a few basic guidelines in mind.

- Make the border no more than three feet wide if you can reach it from only one side; four or five feet if you can get to it from both sides.
- Use harmonizing colors; don't stick plants in willy-nilly.
- To avoid the confetti effect, plant several of the same thing, rather than a series of individual plants.
- Remember that on any given plant, the flowers are in evidence only a few weeks; so choose with an eye to attractive foliage.
- Use plants of different heights, and arrange them from the most likely viewing perspective: tallest in rear, midsize plants in middle, low ones in front.
- Don't forget the obvious: choose plants that match the sun conditions.
- If the border is against a fence or building, that structure is visually a part of the design. What color is it? Texture? Size?

---

### Top 10 Perennials for Hot, Dry Areas

1. Yucca
2. Sedums, sempervivums
3. Oxeye daisy
4. California poppy
5. Spurge (*Euphorbia*)
6. Lavender
7. Artemisia
8. Russian sage
9. Red hot poker plant
10. Evening primrose

---

# *Planting Perennials*

*From Containers.* In the garden center, you are likely to find perennials in pots, either one-gallon or five-gallon sizes. To plant in your garden, follow the general principles for container planting described in the Planting chapter.

*Bareroot Plants.* If you ordered your perennials from a mail-order nursery, they probably came bareroot. Here too, the basic procedure is as described in the Planting chapter.

Ornamental grasses are a unique kind of perennial: they produce large, usually billowy mounds of foliage in shades of green often tinged with other colors as well. Many have unusual and sometimes dramatic flower stalks. Most are evergreen and maintain their beauty year-round, so their shining foliage may be one of your few bright spots in the dead of winter.

These plants may be new to you, but they are getting a lot of attention from gardeners these days, who love their toughness and graceful looks. Here are a few to consider:

1. Maiden grass. (*Miscanthus sinensis 'Gracillimus'*). Grows to 4 feet tall, with hairy white seed heads.
2. Fountain grass (*Pennisetum*). Several varieties, with interesting plumes of pink, black, purple or white. 3 to 4 feet.
3. Fescue. Several nice varieties, including *F. glauca*, 6 to 8 inches, which produces a tight bunch of fine, powder blue foliage; and California fescue (*F. californica*), evergreen, 2- to 3-foot mounds, with tan flower heads on 5-foot stems.

## Growing Perennials

When you see how easy it is to care for perennials, you'll appreciate how popular they have become. Routine maintenance is pretty simple:

- Fertilize in the early spring, just before the plants are ready to start growing. Fertilize again when they have finished blooming. (Review details in chapter on Fertilizer.)
- Water in summer when ground gets dry, as part of your normal watering chores.
- Pick off the dead flowers, to encourage more blossoms.

One thing you will have to do with taller perennials is stake them, so strong winds don't blow them apart and so the long stems don't flop over. Single stakes made of wood, metal, or bamboo are available at your favorite garden center. Or you can use a strong, slender limb from a tree, with all side branches trimmed off. Several commercial products are designed to provide support for multiple stems.

Be sure to position single stakes right next to the stem; if you have to pull the stem over to reach the stake, you've defeated your purpose.

You can, if you like, leave the stakes in place from year to year; they can serve as a marker so you'll always know where the perennials are when the tops die down. If that seems untidy to you, pull them up and store them until next year. The important point to remember in that case is, be sure to position the stakes early, before the plant gets tall.

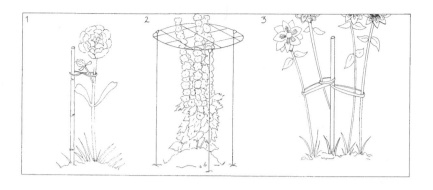

*Tall perennials need staking; here are three types.*

## DIVIDING

Perennials get bigger every year. After a few years, they may outgrow their space in your garden. What is worse, when the roots get too crowded, the plant begins to decline and eventually will stop flowering. What you need to do then is dig the plant up, divide it into several parts, and replant each part as a new plant.

This is a time when gardeners share plants with each other; if you play your cards right, and can arrange to be on hand when a friend is dividing plants, you'll probably come home with some new babies.

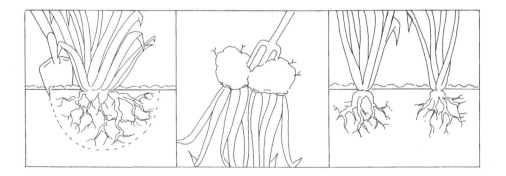

*Dividing perennials keeps them from outgrowing their space and gives you two or more new plants. Dig up the clump and pull it apart with your hands or a garden fork. Replant the two sections individually.*

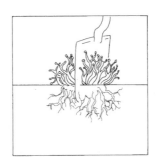

*A quick way to divide a plant is to slice it in half with a shovel and dig out one half.*

The procedure for dividing is not at all difficult; the only tricky part is working up your nerve to do it the first time. New gardeners have difficulty believing it won't hurt the plant. Trust me: not only does it not hurt, the plant really benefits.

Dig the entire plant up, then examine the root structure. If this is a clump with individual segments that you can pull apart with just your hands, do that. If the roots are a tight mass, a garden fork will help tease them apart. A *really* tight clump may need to be sliced in half with a large knife. An alternate technique in that last case is to cut the plant in half while it is still in the ground, using a sharp shovel. Dig up one half and plant it in a new hole, and leave the remaining half in place. New growth will quickly fill in to soften the cut edge.

After dividing, you now have two (or more) plants. Put one back where the original plant was, and put the others in new holes. Or, to keep the garden karma healthy, give some away.

| When to Divide | |
| --- | --- |
| *For* | *Divide in* |
| Plants that bloom in spring | Fall |
| Plants that bloom in early summer | Fall |
| Plants that bloom in late summer | Early spring |
| Plants that bloom in fall | Early spring |

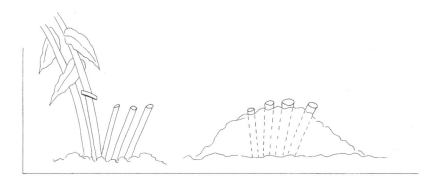

*Wintertime protection for perennials: prune down to 4 or 5 inches and cover with a thick mulch.*

## Winter Protection

In very cold climates, where the ground freezes hard for long periods, you will need to give your perennials some protection. After the first freeze, cut them back to about four inches from the ground, and add a thick layer of mulch: leaves, straw, pine needles, or trimmings from an evergreen tree.

Leaving a few inches of the old stems will help you remember where the perennials are.

*L*eaving aside for the moment seeds and bulbs, all plants come into your life in one of three ways:

1. Bareroot.
2. Balled-and-burlapped, popularly known as B&B.
3. Containers.

Wherever plants are sold—nursery, garden center, variety store, or mail-order company—they have been packaged by the grower or the wholesaler in one of those three ways.

When you order by mail, you do so on faith (see Mail Order chapter for tips); when you are standing among the plants at the garden center, you should check them out carefully and choose the healthiest specimen you can. What to look for depends on which of the three ways it is packaged.

## How to Pick Healthy Plants

### BAREROOT

The roots are indeed bare (that is, not growing in soil) but kept moist in some way. Roses, deciduous shrubs, and many trees are packaged bareroot. The key thing to look for here is that the roots are firm and plump, not all shriveled up. Check the condition of the roots before you buy, if this is possible. In some nurseries, bareroot plants are stored in a bin of damp sawdust or similar material. Make sure you look at the roots of the actual plant that you intend to buy. If the plant has been packaged by a wholesaler, the roots are covered with some moisture-holding material like sphagnum moss and then wrapped in plastic or a cardboard box; at the nursery, you won't be able to see the roots. Check carefully when you get home, and return the plant if the roots are totally dry.

When you order from a mail-order nursery, you usually receive bareroot plants.

### B & B

Young trees, some broadleaf evergreens, and some deciduous shrubs often come this way. The young plants were grown close together in a field, then dug up along with a ball of soil and wrapped in burlap. At the nursery, check to see if there are roots growing out through the burlap. If so, the plant has been confined too long. Pass on buying that one. Press on the ball; it should feel firm, not mushy.

### CONTAINERS

Broadleaf evergreens, conifers, perennials, and annuals all come in containers. Young plants, from a field nursery or greenhouse, have been transplanted into a container filled with soil for ease of shipment.

Look for overall health and vigor—leaves of the right color, a good tight shape with no scrawny stems. Most of all, look for signs of root trouble. If you see roots beginning to circle the top of the pot, or growing out the drainage hole, then the plant has been in that container too long. If you can manage it, slide the plant out of the container and check the bottom of the root ball; if the roots are growing around in a tight, thick circle, skip that plant.

## A Temporary Holding Pattern

Once you get home, if you cannot get them planted right away, place your new plants in a shady, protected spot outdoors. The main thing to avoid is letting the roots dry out. Water containers when the soil feels very dry to the touch. Keep bareroot plants in their packing material (the moss or whatever was used) and keep it damp. Set a B&B plant in the shade and wet the burlap with the garden hose periodically.

An alternative is a technique known as heeling in. It is a little more trouble, but it is safer, because it doesn't depend on you remembering to water. Dig a shallow trench outdoors in a somewhat protected location (near the house, for instance); lay the new plant in sideways and cover the roots with soil. They will keep here for as long as you need, but are easily dug up when you're ready.

---

### Best Weather to Plant

When temperatures are coolish and skies are cloudy and overcast. Pay attention to the forecast: try to plant on a day when the weather will be like that tomorrow too.

# Putting Them in the Ground

In this section basic techniques for planting are described. What packaging each plant comes in determines which technique to use. All plants of the same packaging type are planted pretty much the same way, no matter what they are or how big they are. If there are any special considerations involved in planting a certain type of plant, they will be explained in detail in the related chapter. In all cases, I am assuming that if your soil needed major work, you have already done it (see Soil chapter).

## CONTAINERS

This basic procedure applies to all container plants, from a small six-pack of pansies to large shrubs and trees.

1. Water the plant in its container very thoroughly and let it drain. This helps it slide out more easily, and also eases the transition to its new home.
2. Dig a hole wider and deeper than the container. Set aside the dirt you dug up. If it is heavy clay, mix in some compost, peat moss, or other organic material. (See Soil chapter.) Add some dry or granular fertilizer into the bottom of the hole, and mix it in well.

   If you are planting a whole bed of annuals, loosen the soil throughout the bed with a garden fork or a cultivator. Remove any stones, break up any clods of dirt. Work in some organic material.

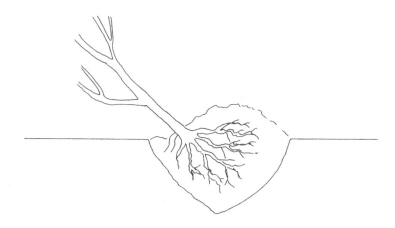

*Plants are heeled in as a temporary measure when you can't plant them immediately; covered with soil, the roots will not dry out.*

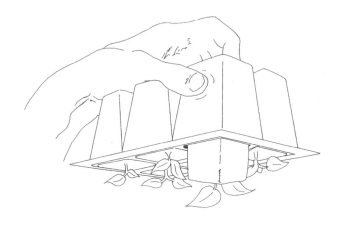

*Thin plastic packs often release their plants if you merely squeeze the sides.*

3. Slide the plant from the container, soil and all. If it does not come out easily, loosen around the edges with a knife, or hold the container upside down and tap the rim against something solid.

   Annuals often come in small plastic pots or six-packs. Most of the plastic used for these packs is very thin, and you can release the root ball by squeezing the outside.

4. Spread the roots out. If they are thickly snarled at the bottom, you *must* untangle the roots or they will just keep on growing in a circle. Don't be afraid to snip off very long roots.

   Annuals that have been growing in their packs for a long time may have a mat of roots echoing the shape of the container bottom. (See illustrations on pages 7 and 8.) Go ahead and cut away or tear off that mat.

5. Place the plant and its soil ball in the hole. If the base of the plant isn't approximately level with the ground, lift it out and fill in with a bit of the soil you removed.

   For bedding plants, use a trowel to dig small individual holes, or make short trenches that hold several plants.

6. Fill in around the plant with the soil you removed. For very large plants, fill the hole with water when you are halfway done, to settle the roots and the soil. At the end, use some of the backfill soil to shape a rounded wall that creates a sort of moat around the plant. (See illustration on page 135.)

7. Fill the moat with water.

   ### BAREROOT

1. First, open up the box and remove the packing material. Don't panic if you don't see any green leaves; the plant is not dead, just dormant.

2. Soak the root ball in a bucket of water overnight.

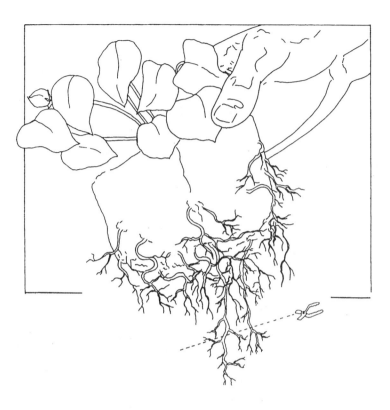

*Spread out the roots before planting the plants. The extra-long roots here should be snipped off.*

### Planting Tip

Here's a technique that works well for me: Soak the entire contents of one tray pack (plants plus their soil ball) in a bucket of water in which you have dissolved a little bit of fertilizer (about 25 percent strength). Let it stay there, to loosen the matted roots, while you dig the holes. After planting, pour the contents of the bucket around the plants, and start a new batch for the next pack.

3. The next day, dig a hole a bit deeper than the root ball and twice as wide as the roots are long.
4. Set aside the soil you dug out and knead it with your hands until it is loose and crumbly. Work in some organic material.
5. Use some of that loose soil to form a volcano-shaped cone in the hole; the top of the volcano should be level with the ground. (See page 137.)

*Basic process for planting containerized plants is now complete: hole has been dug, compost worked into the soil, plant and its soil fitted into the hole. Note the slight wall around the plant. This forms a watering well.*

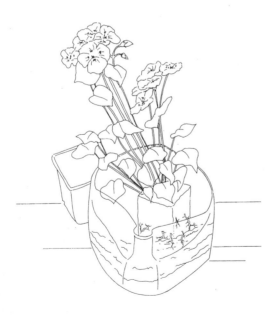

*Presoaking the plant in a very diluted solution of fertilizer helps loosen the roots; here a plastic milk jug has been recycled and cut down into a bucket. After planting, pour the water around the plant.*

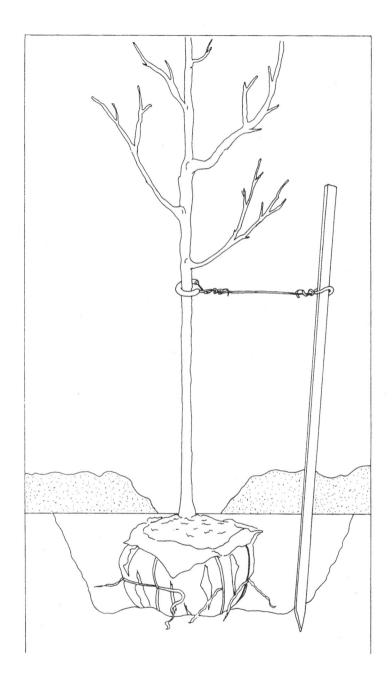

*Balled-and-burlapped plants go into a wide hole. Remove any metal wires but leave the burlap. Backfill with amended soil, water and add mulch. Young trees will need a stake their first year.*

*Gardening from the Ground Up*

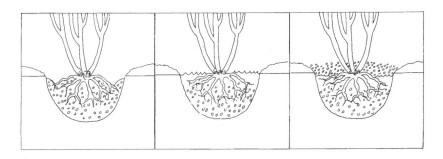

*To plant a bareroot plant, dig a wide hole and form a cone of soil (left). Spread the roots evenly around the cone, then fill in with amended soil (center). Water thoroughly, then add a layer of mulch (right).*

6. Spread the roots over the volcano, distributing them all around.
7. Fill in the empty space with the rest of the removed soil and press it lightly into place, mounding up the edge to create a moat.
8. Water thoroughly; add a layer of mulch.

If you are planting a bareroot tree, your last step is to position a stake and tie the young tree to it; see illustration in chapter on Trees.

Roses almost always come in bareroot form; follow the general process described here, paying particular attention to the location of the bud union (read more about this in chapter on Roses).

### B & B

1. Dig a hole as deep as the root ball and approximately twice as wide.
2. If the soil is sandy, mix it half and half with good topsoil. If soil is very heavy clay, replace it with rich topsoil.
3. Position the plant (still in its burlap) in the center of the hole. Lay a stake or the handle of a shovel horizontally across the hole to verify that the base of the stem is level with the ground.
4. Snip any metal or plastic ties, but leave the burlap in place. You can fold down the top if you like.
5. Fill in the empty space about halfway with the soil you removed, water thoroughly, lightly tamp the soil. Fill in the rest, water, tamp.
6. Add a thick layer of mulch around, but not right up against, the trunk.
7. If this is a tree, position a stake.

## PROBLEMS

*I* must start by confessing my bias. I try very hard to use natural, nontoxic controls for all the trouble spots that inevitably show up in a garden. I do this because I believe that many commercial garden chemicals, especially the poisons, while they may solve a micro-problem, harm the macro-environment, some of them in ways we do not even yet know. I believe that all of us who enjoy watching things grow are honor-bound to protect the soil and the water that nourish them. I also do this because I'd rather spend my money on other things.

I am fortunate to live in a part of the country where this attitude is considered normal and where information and support are readily available. But I do not pretend to be perfect in this regard. This wonderful place where I live, in the state that practically invented recycling, is also blessed with the Garden Pest from Hell: slugs by the bushelful. I confess that on really wet years I succumb to the temptation to poison them, and I do not feel the least bit guilty.

I'm telling you all this by way of a warning: I do not know a great deal about chemical control of insects and plant diseases. If you want picture-perfect plants, with nary a bug in sight, you need another reference book.

However, it is my hope to ease you toward a different way of thinking. When we plant something in a garden, we are deliberately, consciously joining in a natural process. Bugs, bacteria, and weeds are also participants in that process, along with butterflies, hummingbirds, and honeybees. No garden has ever been without problems of some kind. There is no such thing as totally weed-free, pest-free, disease-free; don't make yourself crazy trying to achieve it. The best we can hope for is to keep problems at a low level, so that no real damage is done, and so that the gardening process remains joyful.

# Animal Pests

Deer are an increasing nuisance in urban areas that border their habitat; the more we take over their natural territory, the more they are forced to invade our gardens in search of food.

It is a sad state of affairs, about which any caring person feels bad. But you might not feel so bad when you wake up one morning to find your vegetable garden completely stripped and all your roses chewed off.

Chemical repellents are available, but, as I warned you, I don't use them, so can neither recommend nor not recommend them. Farmers have been known to hang little bags of dog hair around the fence; the scent of dog helps keep deer away. Others tie bags of bloodmeal (a soil amendment) around the garden for the same reason. But your best bet is a fence—a good tall fence. Deer can leap six feet without even trying, and eight feet or more if they are desperate for food.

Moles and other underground critters are very difficult to deal with. They dig tunnels just under the surface of the soil, in the process smashing through the roots of your plants and creating lumps and small mountains of earth all over your lawn.

Chemical controls include poisonous baits and gases that you set to explode down the tunnel. The problem is that these guys are too fast; the gases will just send them to tunnels farther away. The most reliable method is to trap them with a mole trap, set right over the main tunnel.

Other small animals may make themselves known. Rats and field mice can be controlled with traps. Protect young vegetable plants from rabbits with floating row covers (see page 217). If cats use your garden beds as a litter box, plant them their own bed of catnip, far away from your garden.

# Diseases

Plant diseases are caused by bacteria, by viruses, and by fungi. They can be difficult to diagnose, because different diseases produce similar symptoms, and other conditions that are not diseases at all can produce the same symptoms. This section covers just the most common (and most identifiable) ones.

- *Blight.* There are several kinds of blight, with similar symptoms: suddenly the leaves wither and the plant stops growing. Plants infected with fireblight look scorched; other blights first produce what look like water spots on leaves or stems, which later rot.

- *Damping off.* Any one of many fungi can produce damping off, which causes germinating seeds to rot or young seedlings to keel over at the soil line.
- *Leaf curl and leaf blister.* Both these fungus diseases attack leaves, producing yellow bumps or curled, twisted leaves. Serious infestations can kill a tree.
- *Leaf spot.* A fungus disease that causes small dark circles on leaves. One type is black spot, common on roses. Not seriously harmful to the plant, so some people elect to leave it alone.
- *Mildew.* Caused by a fungus, mildew shows up as large white or gray blotches on leaves. Powdery mildew especially affects squashes and cucumbers in the vegetable garden, and roses.
- *Mold.* Fungal disease that produces a black powder on bottoms of leaves; found where aphids are.
- *Rust.* A fungal disease that shows as small orangey spots on the undersides of leaves; very common with roses.
- *Wilt.* There are several kinds of wilt, some bacterial and some fungal. They have the same effect: they cause leaves to wilt suddenly, and eventually the plant dies.

In general terms, the solutions for plant diseases are the same:

1. Prevent them by planting varieties and cultivars that are disease resistant.
2. Be watchful, and prune away all leaves and stems at first sign of infection. Do not add them to compost pile.
3. Keep garden area clean and free of debris.
4. Molds and mildews thrive in damp climates. Provide plenty of air circulation around plants and don't water from above. Don't work with the plants while they are wet.
5. Fungal diseases are difficult to eradicate; spraying with a sulfur fungicide may be your only hope.

## Bad Bugs

The first thing to keep in mind is that many of the insects you see in the garden do far more good than harm. They help aerate the soil, pollinate the flowers, and control harmful insects. And that is the reason that all-purpose, kill-everything-in-sight insecticides are discouraged—they destroy beneficial insects as well as the harmful ones. Not to mention the effect on butterflies, bees, and birds.

Some of the most common good bugs, valuable because they eat the bad bugs, are illustrated on page 121, in the section on organic controls; two others, so familiar you already know what they look like, are ladybugs and praying mantises.

Illustrated here are some of the more common harmful insects.

- *Aphids.* Found most on a plant's newest growth; they love roses and vegetables. Spray off with hose, allow natural predators (lacewings and ladybugs) to do their thing, and use ant traps and barriers to keep away ants that nurture aphids. Use insecticidal soap.
- *Cutworms.* The larvae of moths, they live in the soil and attack plants underground, cutting right through the stem. Put a physical barrier like a ring of cardboard around plants, pushing it partway underground.

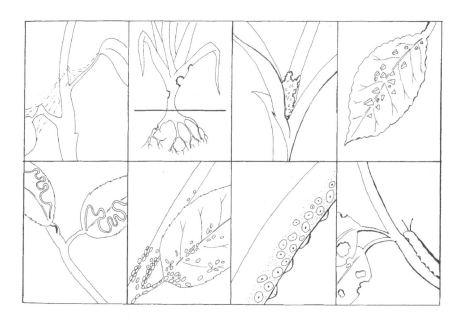

*A rogue's gallery of bad bugs. Top, left to right: Spider mites are too small to see, but leave obvious webs. Cutworms eat stems down near the soil line or just underneath. Mealybugs are white cottony blobs in the joints between stem and leaf. Whiteflies cluster on undersides of leaves. Bottom row: Leaf miners eat their way through a leaf, leaving visible tunnels. Aphids cluster together in tight bunches and suck the juices from the plant. Scale insects are covered with hard brown shells. Slugs and snails feed at night, leaving big holes in foliage.* PROBLEMS

- *Leaf miners.* Tiny larvae tunnel their way through leaves like miners, leaving twisty tunnels. Problematic on leafy vegetables. Floating row covers (see page 217) keep out the flying insects that lay the eggs.
- *Mealybugs.* Common on houseplants. A cotton swab, dipped in alcohol and touched directly on individual insects, is a nontoxic control. A hard hose spray will wash away large colonies.
- *Scale.* Hard shell protects sucking insects underneath from effects of insecticide sprays. Scrape off manually, wash off with a hard hose spray, and set out ant traps and barriers (ants feed on scale secretions as they do on aphid secretions).
- *Slugs.* Set out boards or pieces of cardboard at night; in the morning, scrape off the slugs or snails that collect underneath, dump them into a container of ammonia water. Be on the alert for clusters of eggs (like small pearls) on top of soil or just under the surface, and scoop them up. Apply bait only where pets will not get to it.
- *Spider mites.* You won't see the tiny mites themselves; instead you'll see their webs. Spray the plant with water; wash away the webs; keep it free of dust; raise humidity. Spray with horticultural oil or sulfur for severe cases.
- *Whitefly.* Small wasps are natural predators. Spray infected plants with water or insecticidal soap.

Sensible, environmentally responsible control of insects is a matter of starting with the least toxic solution, progressing toward chemicals only when absolutely necessary. As a very first step, adjust your mindset: decide ahead of time that perfection is not your goal. Then, consider these sequential approaches.

1. Choose plant varieties that are especially sturdy in your area.
2. Keep the garden and all your tools clean. Insects breed in decaying leaves. (Of course this means you will have to give up using organic, leafy mulch. You must decide, based on your specific garden conditions and your patience level, which is more important: weed control or insect control.)
3. Can you remove them by hand? Pick off caterpillars, spray off aphids, drop slugs into a bucket of soapy water.
4. In vegetable gardens, floating row covers (page 217) do a fine job of keeping out flying insects.
5. Encourage beneficial insects by making your garden safe for them with careful environmental controls. Invite them in if they're not already there; you can purchase lacewing and ladybug colonies. *Bacillus thuringiensis*, nicknamed BT, is a bacteria that attacks and kills caterpillars, mosquitoes, and potato beetles. It is sold in garden centers.
6. Read up on some of the homemade remedies for insects; see page 121 for a start.
7. Use less harmful products. Insecticidal soaps and oil sprays (check the shelves

of your favorite garden center) do a good job of eliminating insects, and they leave no residue in the soil.

8. When chemical insecticides are unavoidable, choose the least toxic possible. Pyrethrin is made from plant materials and breaks down into harmless components.

All insecticides (the collective term for chemicals that kill insects) bear a label that lists what they contain and what insects they affect. Read these labels carefully, and apply the product as directed. Learn to be a garden detective. What damage do you see, and what insect is the likely culprit? Don't apply protection against problems you don't have.

An excellent source for help with choosing a course of action is your County Extension office (see page 2). The people there know what insects are prevalent in your area, and they know what works with them.

## Weeds

A weed is any plant that grows where you don't want it to. Weeds are unsightly, but that is not the worst of it. They also rob your plants of water, nutrients, and light.

The best way to get rid of weeds is not to let them get established in the first place. In other words, mulch. Wherever you have a bare spot in your garden, you are inviting weeds. See the chapter on Mulch for mulching materials and application.

Chemicals that kill weeds are called herbicides. The problem is, they kill other plants too and their residue enters the groundwater, affecting a much wider area than you ever intended. Personally, I cannot think of a situation in a garden where they are justified. What you do with weeds is dig them up or mow them down, not poison the soil to eradicate them.

The main thing you want to do is get weeds out of the garden before they set seed. Pulling them up by hand is the surest way to make sure you get everything; it is also extremely satisfying. Easier on your back and knees is a hoe that loosens the soil and slices off weeds. Deep-rooted weeds are stubborn and may come back; digging them out is your only choice. If you can't easily get to them to pull them out, you can kill most weeds by pouring boiling water on them.

**P**ropagation means making a new plant from part of an old one. It is one of a gardener's great joys. With nothing more than a speck of effort on your part and the passage of time, you can have a whole new plant to give away or increase your own garden.

Planting seeds is one very basic method of propagation, but it is covered in its own chapter in this book. Here we look briefly at three other simple propagation techniques: division, cuttings, and layering.

## Division

This involves dividing one plant into two or more smaller pieces by separating it vertically, through the foliage, the base of the plant, and the roots.

You cannot divide plants that have just one main stem. The candidates for division are those that form a large clump of individual plants, or the ones that send up many stems from a thick system of roots. Many perennials fit this description, and, in fact, division is a necessary fact of life for perennials. The techniques are described, with illustrations, in the chapter on Perennials.

## Cuttings

A cutting is just what you would think from its name: a piece of a plant that is cut off from the parent for the purpose of starting a new plant. In fact, sometimes they're called "starts." The basic process is:

1. Remove a tip end of a branch or stem, with at least one node.
2. Place the cutting in something that keeps it lightly damp until it develops roots.
3. Plant the rooted cutting.

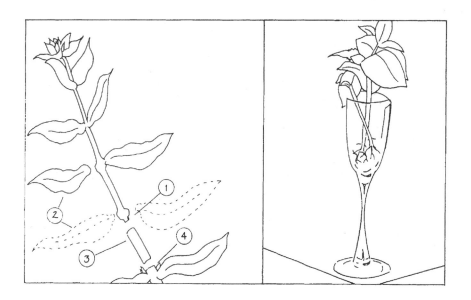

*Stem cuttings from many houseplants root easily. Prune off a section just below a node (#1); remove the leaves from that node (#2) and perhaps the next higher one as well. Remove and discard the bare section of remaining stem (#3), freeing the buds at the next node (#4) to open up into new branches. The cutting, in a glass of water, will form roots at the nodes.*

I'll bet you have seen this done, or perhaps done it yourself, with houseplants, most of which root easily in water. The same principles apply when making cuttings from other kinds of plants as well, although they generally take longer.

Let's look at the three steps a little more closely.

1.  A node is the place on a stem where new growth cells are concentrated; leaves, branches, and roots originate from nodes. Nodes are usually visible as slightly thicker areas on the stem. On many houseplants, you can already see the nubs of roots developing there. Using scissors or a hand pruner, snip right below a node. If there are leaves emanating from that node, strip them off.

2.  What you want to do is keep the end of the cutting moist until the roots start to form, otherwise it just dies before anything happens. Many houseplant cuttings root in a plain old glass of water. Most outdoor garden plants take longer and need something with more substance to hold the cutting steady while roots are forming.

    Any kind of solid soil matter that is both porous (for good air circulation)

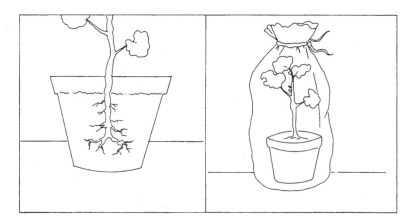

*Stem cuttings will also root directly in a pot, eliminating the need to transplant it later.*
*A clear plastic covering creates a greenhouse effect, speeding up the rooting process.*
*Tie the plastic loosely, allowing for some air circulation.*

and retains moisture works well, as long as it is sterile. Two good rooting mediums are a mixture of sand and peat moss, or perlite and peat moss (read about them in the chapter on Houseplants). What does not work so well is dirt from the garden; it's too dense and heavy, and it could contain harmful bacteria or diseases that will kill the cutting.

Cuttings from a plant with hard woody stems take longer to root. You can give yourself extra insurance for success by using a rooting hormone. This hormone, in powder form, is sold in garden centers. Pour out a small amount into a cup or bowl, and dip the cut end before you place the cutting in the rooting medium.

The rooting process happens more quickly in environments that are warm and humid. That's why commercial growers depend on greenhouses. You can duplicate those conditions at home by covering the cutting loosely with clear plastic, creating a mini-greenhouse. Use a pencil or a chopstick to keep the plastic up off the cutting, and leave a bit of opening for air circulation.

3. When you root cuttings in glass, you know when they're ready—you can see the roots. With rooting medium, you can't tell by looking. Grasp the cutting right at the soil line and pull upward very gently. If it comes right up, it isn't rooted. If there is resistance, it's ready.

The advantage of using a solid rooting medium over water is that you can plant the entire bundle, soil and all, directly into the garden and thus minimize transplant shock.

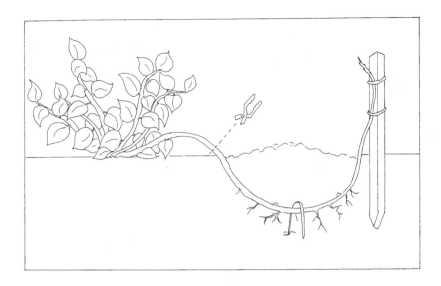

*Layering is a way of propagating a new plant by rooting a long stem while it is still attached to the mother plant.*

## Layering

Layering works with plants that have long, flexible stems. In brief, it involves laying a stem (still attached to the plant) on the ground and forcing a node into contact with soil by burying part of the stem.

Choose a branch that is low to the ground. Dig a hole nearby, bury a midsection of the stem, and leave the outer end exposed. Use something like a brick, a rock, or a bent piece of wire to hold the buried part in place until roots form, and then cut the rooted baby away from the mother plant.

To increase chances of success, cut a short slit in the part of the stem that will be buried and insert something like a match or a short stick to keep it open. Then proceed as before.

Do this operation in the spring, when the plant is about to put on a growth spurt. By fall, the layer has probably rooted. Pull on the exposed part; if it doesn't come right up, it's ready. With a sharp pruner, cut the umbilical cord near the buried part. Dig up the new plant and transplant it to its new home.

**PRUNING**

*O*f all the tasks in a garden, I suspect pruning unnerves people the most. It is not as difficult as you fear, or as mysterious. For one thing, plants are much, much tougher than we give them credit for. How many times have you seen in the forest a tree from which a limb has broken off in the wind? It wasn't "pruned" correctly, but the tree recovered. For another, if you understand a little about how plants grow, you will be able to figure out the basics of pruning anything. So let's take a moment for a short refresher course in basic botany.

## How Plants Grow

1. *Plants grow from the top, not the bottom.* Here's a way to remember that. Imagine you drive a nail into a tree trunk at eye level. Come back in five years and the tree may be six feet taller, but the nail is still in the same place, still at eye level. (The exception to this rule is lawn grass, which pushes new growth from the bottom, which is why mowing it does not change its basic shape.)

2. *New growth begins with buds at the outermost ends of the plant.* This growing tip is called the "terminal bud" or "apical bud," meaning it is at the apex. Buds lower down on the stem are called "lateral." They often are formed in the V where a branch or leaf is attached; the V itself is called the "axil," and so buds that form there are sometimes called "axillary buds."

   In some plants, the terminal bud completely suppresses all the buds lower down on the stem; they will have a chance to open up only if the apical bud is removed. This trait is called "apical dominance." In other plants, lower buds will open on their own, producing branches that ultimately have their own terminal buds. But even in this latter instance, the lateral buds will grow more vigorously if the terminal bud above them is removed.

*When the leading edge of a branch or stem is removed, growth lower down is stimulated.*

3. *Removing growth above a bud will cause that bud to open.* This brings us to the heart of pruning: even though in many plants the lower buds will eventually grow on their own, if we cut away the stem section above a bud, it will *always* open. To put it another way: ***Pruning stimulates growth.***

4. *The new stems will grow in the direction that the bud was pointing.* So you can control the line of new growth by your choice of bud.

5. *Buds are formed on the plant at different times.* That is, some plants set their buds in the summer, some in the fall, some in the spring. This is mostly important for flowering plants.

    The gardener's lingo for this is "old" or "new wood"—"wood" being the stems. "Blooms on new wood" means from buds formed on stems that grew

*Pay attention to the direction the bud is facing. The new branch that develops here will grow toward the left.*

this year; "year-old wood" and "two-year-old wood" mean this year's flowers occurred from buds that formed on the stems from last year or the year before.

What this means is, your timing has to be right. If you have a shrub that flowers in the spring and then sets flower buds in the summer for next year, and if next year you come along and prune it in early spring, you will not have flowers that year because you removed all the flower buds. Unfortunately, there is no easy rule of thumb for this; you have to learn the particulars for each plant you're interested in.

## Pruning Fundamentals

All that botany can be condensed into just a few fundamental principles of pruning.

1. To get a dense, bushy plant, remove its terminal buds.
2. To get a tall, slender plant, remove its lateral buds.
3. Don't prune away the part of the plant you're interested in.
4. Because pruning stimulates growth, you don't want to do it before cold weather, or the new growth will freeze.

# The Golden Rule of Pruning

If ever you're not sure what to do about pruning a particular plant, don't do anything. Leave it to develop its own shape in its own time.

The whole point of pruning is to help the plant achieve its best, to enhance and highlight its natural form, not to make it into something it isn't. If you find that you are continuously pruning a plant that is growing too big for its space, you put it in the wrong spot to begin with. If every year you prune a shrub to get rid of its cascading branches and give it a more rounded shape, you should have put in a rounded plant in the first place.

---

*The First Law of Pruning*
When in doubt, leave it alone.

---

# Two Kinds of Pruning

All the pruning you will ever do on all kinds of plants is one of two kinds: thinning or heading back.

- *Thinning* means removing whole branches (or stems, canes, or whatever). The purpose is to make the plant more open, for better light and air circulation, and also to improve its appearance.
- *Heading back* means removing the growing tips of all the branches. This has the effect of making the plant bushier, more compact—the opposite of thinning.

  "Pinching" is one form of heading back. That means removing the growing tip when the stem is so soft you can pinch it off with your fingers. Pinching is what you do to houseplants to keep them from getting leggy (see Houseplant chapter for illustration), and it is what you do to basil plants to make them bushy.

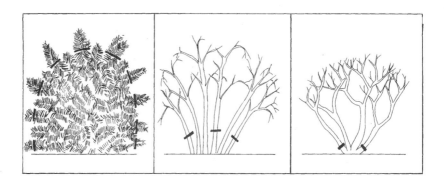

*Pruning for three different purposes. Heading back (left) maintains a rounded shape and promotes thick, bushy growth. Shrub in middle has been neglected; growth is scraggly, all at the top. The three severely pruned stems will fill in with new growth. Thinning (right) completely removes some stems, to open up the plant.*

## When Pruning Isn't Pruning

In this chapter we are talking about pruning deliberately undertaken to amend or enhance the shape of a plant. Other garden tasks that produce similar effects are deadheading, cutting flowers, and cleaning up problems.

*Deadheading* is the name for the process of removing flowers that have faded but are still held on the plant. We deadhead dried flowers because they are unsightly, and because we want the plant to make more flowers instead of going to seed. On the other hand, if you do want the plant to make seeds, leave the dead heads alone.

*Cutting flowers* for flower arrangements is also a form of pruning, when you think about it, for it has the effect of encouraging the plant to make more flowers.

*Cleanup* is an ongoing process. No matter what other kinds of esthetic pruning you do, you should *always* cut away:

- Dead or diseased branches or stems.
- A branch that is rubbing against another branch.
- A branch that is broken.
- Suckers and watersprouts.

*This poor tree has all sorts of common problems that require pruning. Always prune away one of two branches that rub together (#1), overcrowded branches (#2), old stubs (#3), broken limbs (#4), water sprouts (#5), suckers (#6), or a limb that's trying to become another trunk (#7).*

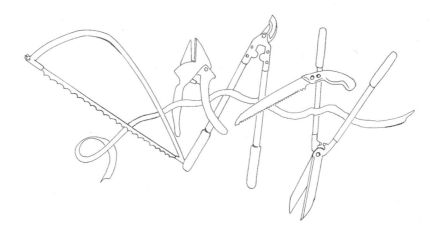

*A collection of pruning tools. Left to right: bow saw for large limbs, hand pruners for everything in the garden, loppers for branches too large for the pruners, a folding saw (for carrying in your pocket), and hedge clippers.*

## Good Tools

The choice of pruning tool is related to the size of the piece you are cutting off.

- Good quality hand pruners are every gardener's most used tool. Many people carry them in a holster, so they will always be handy, and snip away at every opportunity.
- Larger branches that can't easily be cut with hand pruners need a pair of long-handled loppers.
- A pruning saw or bow saw is needed for removing limbs of trees or large shrubs.
- Anything larger than that calls for a professional.

As with all your garden tools, buy the best you can afford and take good care of them. Clean, sharpen, and oil them at the end of the season, and store them away from the weather.

Specific information on pruning houseplants and roses is included in their chapters.

*I*n my opinion, raised beds rank right up there with sliced bread and indoor plumbing. It's an amazingly simple concept that always works—the world needs more things like that.

At its simplest, a raised bed is merely a garden area—large, small, or in between—in which the soil has been mounded up so that it is a few inches higher than the surrounding terrain. Slightly more complex, but longer lasting, are beds contained within a rigid structure.

Often associated primarily with vegetable gardens, raised beds also work just as well with flowers and other landscape plants. Berms, those ridges of earth used by landscape architects as space dividers, are one form of raised bed.

The advantages of raised beds are significant indeed:

- The soil in them is warmer; as much as four or five degrees, which can really make a difference when you're trying to grow warm-season plants.
- You can plant more thickly, because you don't need to leave room for paths between rows, so you get more use out of your space. As a consequence of thicker plantings, you use proportionately less water and less fertilizer, and have fewer weeds. (This is primarily valuable for vegetable gardeners.)
- Simply by force of gravity, they make the soil drain better. If you didn't do anything but raise the level, you would make great improvements in your garden because of the effect on drainage. But usually you also amend the soil as you go, working in organic material or compost while you build up the bed.

All beds should be of a breadth that permits you easily to reach into the middle from one side or the other. This produces another very real advantage: since you never walk on the soil in a bed, it doesn't get compacted. That means less work for you in future years.

Another advantage, more psychological than anything else: a bed creates a separate, defined area. It is easier to calculate (and remember) how many square feet you have in

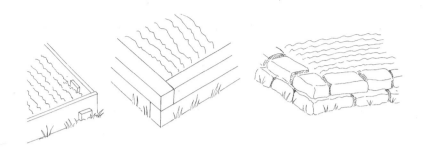

*Raised beds can be bordered in lumber (left), landscape logs or old railroad ties (center), bricks, or stones (right).*

your beds, so you know how much manure or whatever else to buy. It is also, for me, easier and more satisfying to work in a structured unit of space; when you finish weeding one bed, you know it. If you have to stop there, you can at least measure your accomplishment.

## Constructing the Raised Beds

While a raised bed without structural support will work just fine, eventually the rains will break down the soil edges. For a more permanent system, you need to construct a bed with sides. In effect, these are bottomless boxes with sides made of some building material: wood, stones, concrete blocks, or brick.

Any kind of rigid material will work. I once saw a very clever and economical arrangement that used long pieces of corrugated fiberglass rescued from an old patio roof.

The illustrations above demonstrate two of the most common types of wood bed: dimension lumber and railroad ties (actual or reproduction). The best wood is either cedar or redwood, both of which are naturally water resistant. From large garden centers and lumber yards you can also buy what is called "outdoor wood," which has been treated to make it resistant to rotting. Make sure the chemical used for this treatment is not toxic; especially avoid wood treated with pentachlorophenol, called "penta." This caution is important for the sake of a healthy environment, and absolutely critical if you're making beds for plants you intend to eat.

Brand-new railroad ties are saturated with fresh creosote, which is toxic to some plants; buy only used ones. In lumberyards and large garden centers, you can also find outdoor wood milled to look like logs. Very handsome beds can also be made from stones.

### A Special Kind of Raised Bed

Here's the problem: You want to try your hand at growing peonies, and you'd like to construct a new bed for them. But you can't bear the prospect of double digging the area (and who can blame you; see page 199).

Here's what you do: mark out the dimensions of your peony garden, then thoroughly and completely cover it with organic material: grass clippings, shredded leaves, compost, pine needles, everything you can get your hands on. Make the pile at least two feet high. Keep adding to it as it shrinks from decomposition and the rain breaks it down.

When the organic material starts to decompose to humus, add in some good topsoil, or soil from elsewhere in your garden that you have amended with peat moss or compost.

After a few months, whatever was underneath the first layer—grass, weeds, bare dirt—is history, and your new raised bed is formed, all in a few easy steps.

*N*o, it's not a place where you grow pretty rocks. A rock garden is a special type of garden planted on a slope; it uses large rocks to help hold soil in place and features small, low-growing plants that creep and splash over the rocks. In a mature garden, the rocks may be entirely covered by the plants.

You might decide to put in a rock garden because the idea of running a lawnmower over steeply sloping terrain is daunting, or simply because you'd rather have flowers and pretty foliage than grass.

## Top 10 Rock Garden Perennials

1. Creeping phlox
2. Pasque flower
3. Variegated thyme
4. Creeping veronica
5. Hen and chicks
6. Sun rose (*Helianthemum*)
7. Ice plant
8. Alyssum "Basket of Gold"
9. Lewisia
10. Coral bells

Begin by preparing the soil very thoroughly. Make sure it is loose and crumbly; break up all clods of dirt. Work in a good amount of organic material and a complete fertilizer. When you're finished, the soil should be darned near perfect.

Of course this should always be your goal when planting a new bed, but it's particularly critical with rock gardens because once you get the rocks in position it's going to be hard to do any work in the little pockets of soil around them.

Scoop out depressions and place the rocks in them, partially burying them. Behind each rock, shape the soil into a small ledge; this is where a plant will go. In effect, you create a series of miniature terraces, so that when you water this garden, water pools briefly around the plants instead of running down the hill.

*Rock gardens, beautiful in their own right, are wonderful solutions to steep slopes vulnerable to erosion.*

Many kinds of plants work well in rock gardens: shrubs, perennials, annuals, even dwarf forms of trees. The only criterion is that they should be small. Most will be low-growing in form, the better to tumble prettily over the rocks. For vertical contrast, put in some small bulbs: crocuses, snowdrops, miniature daffodils, etc.

| Top 10 Rock Garden Annuals |
|---|
| 1. Dwarf marigolds |
| 2. Moss rose (*Portulaca*) |
| 3. Livingstone daisy |
| 4. Gazania daisy |
| 5. Sweet alyssum |
| 6. Dwarf snapdragons |
| 7. Lobelia |
| 8. Dwarf carnations (*Dianthus*) |
| 9. Verbena |
| 10. Annual periwinkle (*Vinca*) |

## MAINTAINING YOUR ROCK GARDEN

After the first year, you won't have much trouble with weeds; the rocks and the spreading plants effectively keep them away. But two chores that always need your attention are fertilizing and pruning. Rock gardens seem to need continuous tidying up. If you have planned your garden well, you'll have flowers from early spring through late summer. Keep picking off the dead flowers. Rock gardens tend to be planted tightly and in a concentrated space. A little bit of overenthusiastic growth that would be tolerable in a large bed could be a real problem here, for the neighboring plants can be completely overrun. Keep your pruners at the ready.

When they start to bloom, and all through the growing season, flowering plants will need a boost of fertilizer. You can't really get to the soil to work in compost as you could in other, more spacious parts of the garden, so you will have to apply liquid or granular fertilizer that you can sprinkle right around the plants.

### Bulbs for the Rock Garden

1. Species tulips
2. Miniature daffodils
3. Crocuses
4. Fibrous begonias
5. Border dahlias
6. Snowdrops
7. Rhodohypoxis

**C**ards on the table: roses are not easy.

Some would question whether they even belong in a book for beginners. Ultimately I decided yes because roses are so popular and so many people want to know about them; how could we ignore a plant that has been the world's favorite flower for 5,000 years?

The hardest part of *growing* roses is not the pruning, which seems to spook people, but dealing with the harmful insects and the diseases. (More on that shortly.) The hardest part of *learning about* roses is coming to grips with all the confusing classifications.

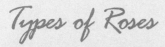

## Types of Roses

Roses have been enjoyed in gardens for thousands of years and have been actively cultivated for almost as long. There are more than 200 species of roses and quite literally thousands of cultivars. A recent interest in old-fashioned roses has brought many of the older varieties back to market, and meanwhile hybridizers are still hard at work developing new beauties to introduce.

Reading about roses in books and catalogs, one could very easily become overwhelmed by the names of categories and subcategories, but let's try to keep some perspective: the names are not important in themselves, but only as a convenient device for communicating information. Mail-order catalogs group their offerings by category, and reference books present growing information by category. You don't have to know, or grow, every kind there is, but you will find it useful to be aware of the major categories.

Most reference books group roses into three large divisions, reflecting their historical era:

### MODERN ROSES

These roses date from 1867, the year the first hybrid tea rose was introduced. Modern roses are hybrids (a cross between two types). Their botanical characteristics have been either accentuated or downplayed by hybridizers, so that now the new versions are resistant to certain diseases, extra hardy in cold weather, have especially large flowers, and so forth. Modern roses have spectacular blossoms and bloom for a long period. The focus is almost completely on the flowers; in contrast, the character of the plant itself is inconsequential (an exception is the shrub rose). Most of the roses you see in home gardens are modern types.

Included in this overall category are these types:

- *Hybrid teas.* This is the most popular type of rose by far, the ones with long stems and individual flowers. Long-stemmed roses from the florist are hybrid teas. It is a cross between a tea rose and a hybrid perpetual, two "old" roses (see page 163).
- *Polyantha.* The flowers are arranged in clusters at the ends of stems, rather than singly. Individual flowers are small.
- *Floribunda.* Also a cluster type, with medium flowers. Floribundas are a cross between hybrid tea and polyantha roses.
- *Grandiflora.* This cross between hybrid tea and floribunda roses is relatively recent: 1954. Grandifloras are often grouped together with hybrid teas, which they resemble in many respects.
- *Shrub roses.* This group includes many species that share a certain pattern of growth: larger than the four types above (which are collectively called "bush" roses), with more foliage—in other words, more like a shrub than a rosebush. As a group they tend to be hardy, disease-resistant, and not demanding about pruning.
- *Climbing* and *rambling* roses are very similar. Both produce very long and pliable stems that can be trained to a wall or trellis. Ramblers are a bit more flexible and are therefore easier to train, but functionally these two are the same.

- *Patio* roses are like floribundas but much smaller overall; 2 to 3 feet tall.
- *Miniature* roses are just that—miniatures of hybrid teas and floribundas, 1 to 2 feet in height.

### OLD ROSES

Also called "heritage" and "antique," old roses are those that predate the ones in the modern group. They were first cultivated hundreds of years ago by rose breeders in Europe and in the East, and recently have enjoyed a resurgence of interest. As a group, they tend to be much more fragrant than modern roses and have more graceful lines. These two qualities endear them to contemporary rose lovers, which is why many are now being offered again by nurseries. The main types of old roses are:

| | |
|---|---|
| Alba | Bourbon |
| Centifolia | China |
| Damask | Gallica |
| Hybrid musk | Hybrid perpetual |
| Moss | Noisette |
| Portland | Tea |

Each of these types has its own special characteristics, and each contains many, many species.

### SPECIES ROSES

These are the roses that grow wild, bred only by Mother Nature without assistance from humans. The term is also applied to species roses and species hybrids produced for market. That is, you can buy a rugosa rose, which is one species, from a rose nursery; you don't have to search the world over to find it growing in a field somewhere. Species roses are large shrubs, with arching branches and fragrant flowers; they usually bloom just once, rather than over and over in a season.

Incidentally, in Europe they use a somewhat different and, to my mind, infinitely more sensible classification system:

- Large-flowered bush roses (hybrid teas and grandifloras)
- Cluster-flowered bush roses (floribundas)
- Dwarf cluster-flowered (patio)
- Miniature, climbing, rambling, and shrub—same as in the American system.

## Buying Roses

In the garden center and also in mail-order catalogs, you will most often find roses packaged as bareroot plants. (Roses are also sold in containers, and miniatures always come this way.)

Choosing good roses is made easier by becoming familiar with three rating systems.

1. Bareroot plants are graded #1 (the highest), #1½, or #2, depending on how many stems (called "canes") they have; the more canes, the faster and sturdier they will grow.
2. Certain rose test gardens all around the country test new cultivars for two years. Those judged to be outstanding are designated as "All America Rose Selection" by the nonprofit AARS organization. Plant labels and mail-order catalog entries specify the AARS roses.
3. The nonprofit American Rose Society evaluates rose varieties and gives them a number rating from a low of 1 to a high of 10. Their excellent little handbook, published each year, is an index to all roses by classification and color; the entries include the numbered ratings. The handbook (see Appendix) also lists AARS winners and the award winners from ARS's own test gardens.

One characteristic of roses that will probably be important to you as you choose your selections is whether the particular species blooms just once in a season, or blooms several times (the rosarian's term is *reblooming*), and if it blooms once, how long the blooming period lasts. Specialty nurseries usually include this information in their catalogs.

## Top 10 Roses

1. Mozart. A hybrid musk that grows vigorously and is practically indestructible. No fragrance, but luminous dark pink flowers rebloom four times during summer. 4–5 feet tall, 6–7 feet across.
2. Hansa. A rugosa hybrid with rich green leaves that are crinkly, like all rugosas. Fluorescent deep pink flowers form rosehips the size of cherry tomatoes. Six feet tall and very thorny, so makes a good hedge plant.
3. Madame Isaac Pereire. A Bourbon rose with large and deliciously fragrant deep pink flowers; reblooms many times. Four feet high with long arching canes that can be trained to climb.
4. Westerland. A very large shrub rose (6 feet high and wide), with large flowers in a color that is hard to describe: orange and yellow bleed into each other like an abstract watercolor. The color is magnetic, draws your eye from a distance.
5. Veilchenblau ("veil of blue"). This climbing rose blooms just once, for about two months; small, cute, almost purple flowers in clusters. Delicious fruity scent. Prefers partial shade.
6. Bonica. A shrub rose with medium pink flowers that rebloom all summer. Foolproof plant survives standing water and all kinds of neglect. Four feet tall and 5 across, could be used for medium hedge.
7. *Rosa glauca.* This species rose has burgundy leaves, pink flowers, then hips that start out maroon and then turn orangey-red. Blooms once, for about a month. Six feet tall and 8 feet across, with arching canes. Nice as a specimen or backdrop.
8. Scarlet Meidiland. A shrub rose (4 feet tall by 8 across) that tolerates partial shade. Clusters of small flowers in a true red color; reblooms throughout summer.
9. New Face. A large shrub rose (6 feet tall by 8 wide) with clusters of reblooming creamy yellow flowers edged with pink. Very vigorous, tough, carefree.
10. Penelope. A hybrid musk, 5 feet tall and 5 wide. Bears clusters of lightly fragrant flowers that seem creamy pink in some light, pale yellow in others. Reblooms many times.

    *Note:* This Top 10 list was contributed by garden designer and writer Barbara Ashmun, who gardens in Portland, Oregon, known as the City of Roses. For those of you who yearn for a classic rose-looking rose, I have added one more to Barbara's list.
11. Double Delight. A hybrid tea with large flowers that show two distinct colors on each petal: creamy yellow with red edges. AARS winner.

# Planting Roses

Almost all modern roses are what is known as "budded plants": The roots from one species that has a strong root system but unspectacular flowers are grafted onto the top of another species that has stunning flowers. The place where the two join is called the "bud union," an obviously thicker, knobby section of stem at the base of the canes. The position of that bud union is important in planting.

Container roses can be planted any time the ground is not frozen. Bareroot plants should go in the ground in January or February, unless winter temperatures of 10° or below are common in your area, in which case fall or early spring is better. The idea is to give the plant time to establish strong roots before the growing season begins.

Planting a rose is similar to planting any bareroot plant (see Planting), but there are a few additional points to remember.

1. Choose your location: full sun, well-drained soil. If you're planting several, space them 2 to 4 feet apart. Roses like a lightly acidic soil, around pH 6.5 (see Soil chapter for explanation of pH). If you have reason to suspect your soil is much different from that, do a pH test and take remedial action if it is one full unit off. And if your drainage is awful (see Soil), grow your roses in raised beds.

2. Unwrap the plant and remove the packing material. Prune off any scraggly-looking roots or any that seem to be dead. Check the canes; often growers trim them all to the same length, regardless of where the buds are. Prune each cane back to a bud (see illustration on page 173). Set the plant in a bucket of water to soak, at least an hour ahead of planting.

3. Dig a hole 18 inches wide. Work in some compost or other organic matter and a complete fertilizer. Form a mountain of soil in the center of the hole and spread the roots evenly around it.

4. Lay a stick (or shovel handle) across the hole as a visual guide to the level of the surrounding soil. The bud union should be about an inch higher; if it is not, move the plant aside and adjust the height of the mountain. (Some gardeners in extremely cold regions have better success positioning the union 1 inch below soil level.)

5. Fill in the hole with the soil you removed, tamp it lightly, and water thoroughly.

6. Mound up a protective hill of soil or mulch around the plant; use soil you took from another spot in the garden. Over the next few weeks, gradually (and carefully) remove this mound as the plant starts to grow. (If you planted the rose in the fall, leave this mound in place through the winter.)

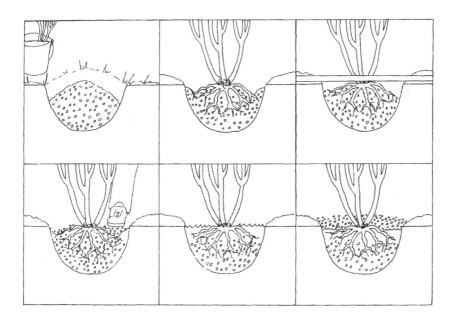

*Six steps to planting a bareroot rose: Soak the roots in a bucket of water while you dig the hole and form a cone of amended soil. Spread the roots over the cone. Use the handle of a shovel to make sure the bud union is at the right level with the soil. Backfill and lightly tamp the soil. Water thoroughly. Pile mulch around base of plant.*

Planting container roses is like planting from any container (see chapter on Planting). Make sure the bud union is at the same level in the ground as it was in the container.

# Caring for Your Roses

Roses need a lot of water. Water the plants slowly and deeply; get the soil wet down to 18 inches. Keep a good layer of organic mulch around the plants to hold in moisture.

They also, like all heavy bloomers, need regular fertilizing. Fertilize about a month after you first plant them, and again in early spring if they are the type that blooms only once, three to four times during the season if they bloom over a long period.

While the roses are blooming, deadhead regularly to keep the flowers coming.

> **"Rose Sickness"**
>
> If you already have an established rose bed and wish to add new plants to it, dig deep holes for them but use soil from another spot in the garden as your backfill. The older roses create a soil condition that keeps the new ones from growing; it is known as "rose sickness." Honest.

## Winter Protection

If it routinely dips below 20° in the winter where you live, your roses will need some kind of protection against the cold.

1. Let the last flowers stay on the plant to form rosehips; this will send a signal to the plant to stop producing new growth cells.
2. Stop fertilizing six weeks before the first killing frost date (see Weather chapter for explanation of frost dates).

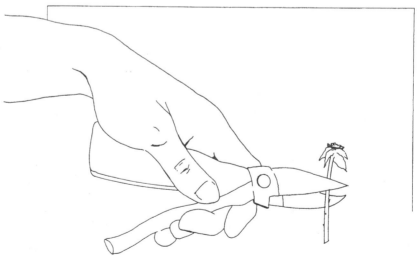

*Roses are one of the plants that benefit from constant deadheading, to keep new flowers forming.*

3. Cut the canes back to 2 to 3 feet, or approximately half their height.
4. Make a protective mound of soil (from somewhere else in the garden) around the base of the plant. When that mound freezes, cover it with a thick layer of mulch and add something (burlap, wire) to hold the mulch in place. You want to keep the soil from repeatedly freezing and then thawing.
5. If your winter temperatures drop to 0° and below, give the plants extra protection: Make a cylinder of chicken wire around each plant and fill it with mulch material.
6. Normally you leave the long canes of climbers in place; cover the base of the plant with mulch and burlap. If below-zero temperatures are common, untie the canes from their support, lay them on the ground, and cover them with soil and mulch.

When ordering or purchasing roses, pay attention to their hardiness rating; choose varieties that work in your area, and you'll save yourself a lot of winter worries.

## Problems

Roses are highly susceptible to two insect pests—aphids and spider mites. Aphids are tiny green things that *looooove* the new buds and growing tips of the plant; in a thick infestation they will be clambering all over each other (see illustration on page 141). They suck the juices from the plant and will eventually kill or seriously maim it. A very hard spray from the garden hose will sometimes be enough to knock them off. See the chapter on Organic Gardening for other non-toxic methods of controlling them. If you are so inclined (or if you are desperate), spray them with an insecticide recommended for aphids.

Spider mites show up when the weather gets hot; you will see their webs on the backs of leaves and in the notches between leaf and stem (see illustration on page 141). They have roughly the same effect on the plant as aphids—a general weakening—and are controlled in similar ways.

And then there are the fungal diseases: black spot, rust, and powdery mildew. You'll know when you have them, for the names tell you what they look like. Rust is a series of rusty red spots on the tops and bottoms of leaves; black spot produces round black circles on the leaves; and powdery mildew shows up as mildew splotches on leaves and a white powdery coating on new flower buds.

All these fungal diseases are hard to control. Good air circulation around the

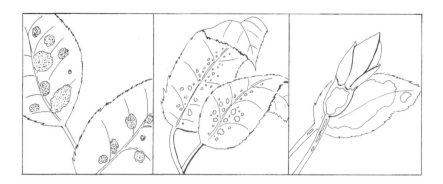

*The three most common, and most insidious, rose diseases.*
*Left to right: Black spot, rust, and powdery mildew.*

plants is very important as a preventive measure. So is a good fall cleanup, disposing of all old foliage at the end of the season. Probably most important of all is choosing disease-resistant varieties to begin with.

But if you didn't do that, and your organic controls don't work, you may decide to resort to chemical fungicides. Use a fungicidal soap spray that contains sulfur; do it while the plant is dormant.

### Get Those Suckers

It sounds like a semipolite swear word, but *sucker* is actually a real botanical term. It's the name for a stem that grows up from underground roots, slightly apart from the main stem of a plant. Suckers tend to drain water, growing energy, and food away from the main plant, and you should remove them. Left to grow, they will eventually take over the main plant.

Removing suckers is important for all roses, and critical with budded roses. The suckers are emanating from the root stock, which will not have especially appealing flowers.

The temptation is to reach down to the soil line and snip these suckers off with your pruners—"Got you, you sucker." But in fact what you have done is *prune* that sucker, and you know what pruning does: stimulates growth. So soon you'll have several suckers in that one spot.

Instead, dig away the soil until you find the spot where the sucker is attached to the root stock. Grab hold near the junction and pull down and away, ripping off the sucker and all its growth buds. That should do it.

# Pruning

Now we come to the part about roses that makes people nervous. Pruning is very important to the production of beautiful flowers, but is not as hard as you think, especially if you remember the general concepts. You might want to review the basics in the chapter on Pruning; here is a summary.

## PRUNING PRINCIPLES

1. Pruning stimulates plants to grow. This means that if you prune shortly before cold weather sets in, you will be encouraging new growth that will probably freeze.
2. Plants grow from the top (or the outer tips), not from the base. Each year's new growth starts where last year's ended.
3. Most plants bloom on new growth; stems left from the previous year will produce new growth out at the end of the stems in the spring, and flowers will appear on the new part. For roses, this means that if old growth is left on the plant, new growth will be weak and flowers puny.
4. Plants want to make seeds, so they can reproduce themselves. Seeds come after flowers. If flowers are removed from the plant before seeds are formed, the plant will produce more flowers.
5. Flower buds show up at certain preset times, and this differs in different plants: some set their buds this year, some last year. If you prune away the flower buds, you won't have any flowers.

We prune roses for maximum flowers. In addition, you should *always* make pruning cuts in these cases:

- To remove dead or broken canes; cut off at the base.
- When two canes are rubbing against each other; remove one.
- When a cane is noticeably thinner and weaker than the others.
- To remove very old and unproductive canes that have not bloomed in several years.

Pruning roses successfully means learning a few key points:

- When to do it (this is a function of how cold it gets where you live and whether the flower buds are set this year or last year).
- Where on the plant to make the cut (this varies according to the type of rose you have and your weather).
- How to make the cut (this is always the same; learn it once and you've got it forever).

Certain rules apply in all situations:

- Always be sure your pruners are sharp.
- Unless you have a specific reason for wanting to fill in the interior (for a hedge, perhaps), always cut just above a bud that is facing outward, not in toward the center of the plant.
- Always make your cut at a 45-degree angle, sloping away from the bud (see illustration on page 173.).
- Always cut back to where the inner part of the cane (the pith) is not dead or diseased. The pith of healthy canes is white or cream colored, not brown. If you have to cut back farther than you planned in order to find healthy pith, do so.
- Always wear gloves.

Because the decisions are different for different types of roses, we'll look at pruning details in categories. (Now you see why it's useful to know about classifications.)

### HYBRID TEAS AND GRANDIFLORAS

The goal with these two types of roses is large, beautiful individual blossoms at the end of long stems. The way to achieve that is to prune them just before they begin to grow after the dormant period in the winter.

These roses produce flowers on new wood (that's the gardeners' term for branches that grow this year). Take another look at pruning principles #2 and #3 on page 171. If you leave the long stems from one year, the next spring the new growth will come from the tips of those old stems. The new growth will not be vigorous, and as a result the flowers will not be large. What you want to produce with pruning is a brand-new stem each spring, which will be vigorous enough to produce stunning flowers.

If winters are severe where you live, you might have cut back all the canes to 3 or 4 feet in the fall to protect them from cold and wind damage. In milder climates, you might not have done this, and the old canes are still as tall as they were at the end of the season. In either case, start checking the canes when the worst of the winter weather is over. This could be late winter or early spring. When the buds start to get fatter, that is your cue: Time to prune.

It might seem hard to imagine at this point, but the buds nearest the cuts will develop into long stems, with more buds and flowers at their tips. Don't visualize that you will end up with a flower right at that point where you cut; that is merely the point where new stem growth will originate.

The question of where on the stem to make the cut is primarily answered by your climate. Where there is a chance of a killing freeze later on, prune high; leave at least

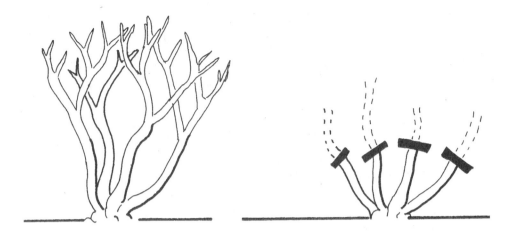

*Prune hybrid tea roses down to several healthy buds in early spring. New strong stems will form, producing vigorous flowers in summer.*

five buds. That way, if a late freeze comes, the top part of the cane will die back but you will (cross fingers) still have some healthy buds lower down, and you'll prune back to that point. In other words, leave yourself some margin for surprises.

On the other hand, if there was a rough winter and all the canes are black, you have to cut down to the base; you have no choice—the tops are dead.

*The perfect pruning cut: just above a bud and sloping away from it, at a 45-degree angle.*

The lower you prune (the shorter the finished product), the longer it will take for the new canes to reach productive size. In warm climates, where roses grow too big, this is an advantage.

When you make your first cut, look at the interior of the stem. If the inner pith is healthy, stop here. If the cane looks dead or diseased, keep going an inch at a time until you hit healthy pith. Do the same with all the other canes. When you're done, you should have four or five strong, healthy canes; the trimmed bush should make a V shape, with lots of open space between canes.

### FLORIBUNDAS AND POLYANTHAS

These cluster-flowered types also flower on new wood. Prune them at the same time—end of dormancy, just as the buds show signs of life. But remember your goal: to produce large sprays of flowers. Rosebushes with lots of stems make more flowers than those with just a few. To get the full, lush look you want with flori-bundas, prune as you would with the large-flowered types described above but leave more canes in place—seven or eight, rather than four or five.

### SHRUB ROSES

Most shrub roses flower on two-year-old growth. If you prune them heavily, you'll be cutting off the part of the plant where the flowers would be—and so you'll have no flowers.

Don't do any pruning at all the first three years of life; after that, cut back only lightly.

Many of these sturdy plants do quite nicely with only minimal pruning for years. If you suspect that an older shrub rose needs rejuvenating (if flower production falls off), plan to do it over a four-year period. Count the number of healthy canes; the first year, prune one fourth of that number (those that appear to be the oldest) down to the ground. The next year, another fourth. And so on. As old canes are taken out, new ones grow. After four years, you'll have a whole new plant. (Always cut away canes that are completely dead; don't include them in your count.)

### SPECIES ROSES

As with shrub roses, species roses don't need a lot of pruning. They send up long, flexible stems that arch over into a graceful fountain shape. Short side shoots develop from those stems after two years, and it is on those shoots that the masses of flowers appear. If you prune these roses heavily, you will get lots of new leaves and hardly any flowers.

Species roses do best if you don't prune them at all. Snip away any broken or dead branches, but otherwise let these beauties go about their rambunctious

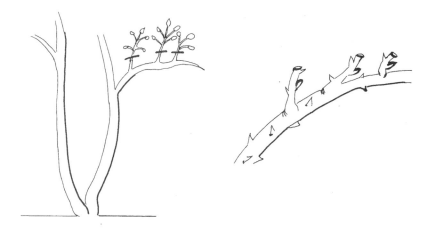

*Climbing roses are pruned after they finish blooming. Leave the long canes intact; prune just the short stems that had flowers on them.*

business. If after many years they seem to be deteriorating, gradually build up new stems in the four-year process described on page 174.

### OLD ROSES

Most old-fashioned roses bloom just once a year, from buds that form on last year's growth. They should be pruned after they have finished flowering; cut stems back to about two-thirds their original length.

### CLIMBING ROSES

Picture how climbing and rambling roses grow, and you'll understand how to prune them. These types produce very long and flexible stems, with many short side stems that bear the flowers. If the long stems were upright, the side stems (called "laterals") would grow out horizontally. But since climbers are usually trained in such a way that the long stems are held horizontally, the short stems actually grow upward.

These roses bloom on old growth, and most bloom just once a year. Therefore, pruning should take place after the flowering has stopped.

Don't do anything the first three years. After that, trim back only the short laterals. Remember: the canes don't bear any flowers, only the laterals. Don't cut back the main canes, the way you would for hybrid teas, or you'll have to wait two more years for flowers.

**SEEDS**

$\mathcal{A}$ seed is a self-contained embryonic plant. The beginnings of everything—roots, stems, flowers, and fruit—are in that one little seed, which may be no bigger than the head of a pin. Pretty darned amazing, when you think about it.

As a matter of fact, within the seed are all the nutrients the plant needs to get started. The seed is dry, which is Mother Nature's way of holding it in limbo until the right weather cycle comes around again. But once it absorbs moisture, and once the temperature is warm enough, that seed will burst open and start making roots, stem, and leaves. It doesn't need fertilizer to do that, it doesn't even need to be in soil. And you couldn't stop it if you wanted to.

Every plant forms a seed of some kind. An acorn is the seed of an oak tree. Pine cones have seeds between the scales (the pine nuts we buy in the grocery store are the seed of a particular type of pine tree). Those cute little propellers that maple trees produce hold the seed in the pilot's position. Holly berries contain seeds for future generations of trees. Rosehips hold rose seeds, and aniseed, which we buy as a spice, is the seed of the anise plant. With enough time and carefully controlled conditions you could, in theory, grow a plant from any of these seeds. But it is a thousand times simpler to buy roses from a mail-order nursery and holly trees from the garden center, and get on with life.

Most people think of seeds in conjunction with annuals—vegetables, annual flowers, and herbs—and that is what we shall be doing in this chapter.

## Where to Get Seeds

Any large garden center will carry a wide selection of seeds from several companies. If you already know what varieties you like, a quick stop at your favorite store may be all you need.

But if you're not sure what you want, you will be better off to write for catalogs and compare their listings. For one thing, you will find a much broader selection, including many varieties you did not know existed. For another, the good catalogs are wonderful learning tools, with specific, detailed growing information. For yet another, looking through them is a heck of a lot of fun.

The Appendix of this book contains a listing of some catalog companies I especially admire. You can find many others, including smaller companies with interesting specialties, among the ads in gardening magazines.

The catalogs are issued early in the year, starting in January. Generally you have until midspring to place your order; if you wait much later than that, some things may be out of stock.

---

### Saving Seeds

Often a packet of seeds has more than you really need for one season. Should you save them until next year? I vote no. Once the package is opened, it's too easy for moisture to get inside, and then the quality of the seed deteriorates. The cost of the seeds is the least of your expenses; don't jeopardize your success next year to save a few pennies.

If you hate the idea of wasting them, buddy up with a friend and place a joint order; each of you gets half of each packet.

---

# Indoors or Out?

The immediate question you will face, once you hold the packet of seeds in your hand, is whether to start them indoors or wait until you can plant them directly into the ground outside. The reason for starting indoors is to give them an early start in a warm environment while it is still too cold for them outdoors.

That decision has partly to do with your temperament, and even more to do with your weather. Starting seeds indoors requires your scrupulous attention. On the other hand, if you have a short growing season and you insist on growing warm-season vegetables, you have little choice.

I emphasize vegetables here because the question is much more critical for them than it is for flowers or even herbs. All plants grown from seed need a certain amount of time to reach the point where they do whatever it is you want them to do. With flowers, if unusually cool weather makes them "late," you'll still get at least some flowers. Same with herbs: you'll be able to harvest a few leaves. But with vegetables, if they aren't growing for the full amount of time needed to produce edible vegetables, you get essentially nothing, and you might as well not have bothered.

Making this decision boils down to an exercise in arithmetic. The seed packet holds a critical piece of information: days to maturity. That is how long the plant needs to grow before it produces marigold flowers or eggplants ready to eat.

The second piece of information you need is the length of the growing season in your area. That is, how many days are there between the last killing frost in the spring, and the first killing frost in the fall? (See more about this in the chapter on Weather.) Get this from your gardening neighbors, from a good nursery, or from that fount of all knowledge, your County Extension office. (It also comes in handy for many garden tasks to know what those two frost dates are, so ask that while you're asking.)

Now compare the two numbers. If the first number is larger than the second, then the plant needs to be growing longer than your growing season allows, and so you need to start the seeds indoors. The amount of difference tells you how far in advance you must do this, at a minimum. You can also start the seeds even earlier than this, growing your seedlings to a larger size indoors before planting them out. But the longer they are grown indoors, the more of your attention is required in the meantime and the more serious the transplant shock when they finally do get planted. As with many other things in gardening, you have to weigh one advantage against another.

## Planting Seeds in the Ground

Planting seeds directly in the ground—it's known as "direct seeding"—is always the best, provided the weather cooperates. This way, seedlings never need to be transplanted, which is always a serious shock to their system and one from which it takes a long time to recover.

1. Prepare the ground thoroughly. If it's a new bed, do the remedial soil work described in the Soil chapter. But even if you planted in this same spot last year, you still have work to do. Seeds need extremely light, loose soil so their fine roots can penetrate. Work the top layer of your soil well. Remove any large clods of dirt you can't break up, dig in some good compost, and rake the top smooth. (See page 179.)
2. Just before planting the seeds, wet the soil well. (If you water the ground after planting the seeds, you run the risk of washing them away.)

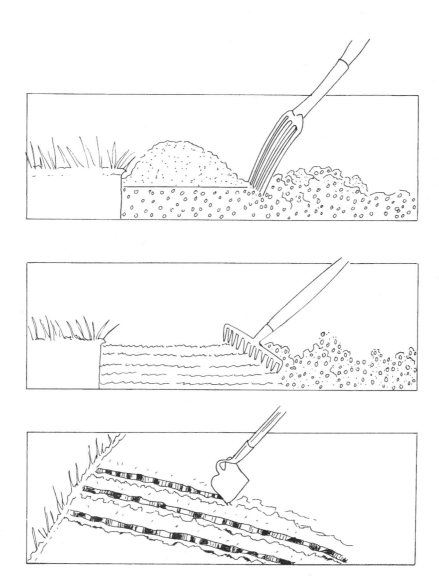

*Getting ready to plant vegetable seeds: Dig soil and incorporate compost (top); rake the surface smooth (center); use the tip of a hoe to dig out shallow trenches in straight rows.*

3.  Plant the seeds. For annual flowers, you may wish to broadcast the seed. Scatter them over the top of the damp soil, then cover them with a light layer of good topsoil or organic mulch.

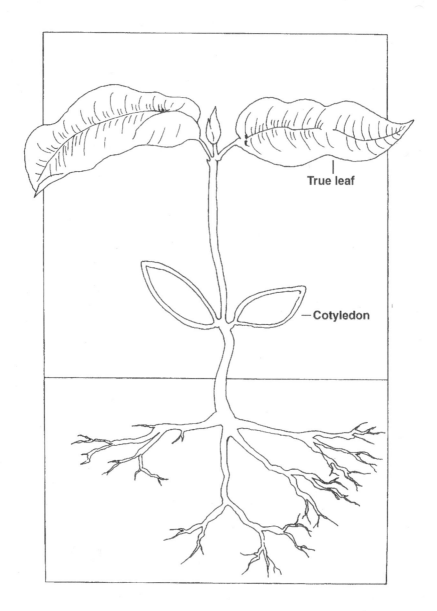

True leaf

Cotyledon

*Anatomy of a seedling. The first to open is the seed coat, the cotyledons. They are not leaves, even though they may look like it. Once true leaves form, you'll see the difference.*

4. Vegetables are often planted in straight rows. Use the handle of a garden tool or a long board to mark the row, then dig out a shallow trench with the edge of a hoe. Drop the seeds in, and push the excavated soil back into place, firming it lightly over the seeds.

---

### Top 10 Easiest Seeds to Start

| *Flowers* | *Vegetables* |
| --- | --- |
| 1. sunflower | 1. radish |
| 2. zinnia | 2. pumpkin |
| 3. stock | 3. bean |
| 4. marigold | 4. pea |
| 5. cosmos | 5. corn |

---

Take another look at the back of the seed packet. It will tell you the germination time: how many days you have to wait before you see any action. Depending how long this is, you may need to water the ground one or more times. Be guided by how dry the soil is and by common sense. Use a very fine spray, so you don't dislodge the seeds.

The first thing you see will be the opened-up halves of the seed coat, called the cotyledons (see page 180). These are not leaves. The true leaves come next. Don't do anything to the young seedlings until they have two sets of true leaves.

The next chore you have is also the hardest: thinning out the baby seedlings; in other words, pulling out and discarding some so that the remaining ones have room to grow. Except for things that have seeds so large you can place them exactly where you want (and there aren't many of those), you surely planted lots of seeds close together. If you do not thin out the tiny seedlings, *none* of them will grow satisfactorily. It is hard to make yourself do this; it feels wasteful and murderous. Do it anyway.

---

### The First Law of Seeds
Thin, thin, thin the seedlings.

---

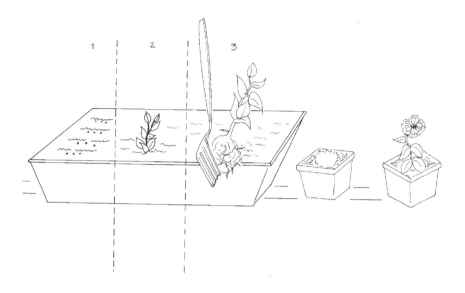

*Sowing seeds in flats. Spread seeds on damp soil (step #1). As they emerge, thin them to strongest seedlings (#2). When they have several sets of leaves, lift them from the flat (#3) and transplant them into larger containers.*

## Starting Seeds Indoors

Inside your home, germinating seeds need a few basics: moisture, light, and warmth.

The temperature that is comfortable for you (around 70 degrees) is sufficient for most seeds; some people use a heating pad under the seedling tray for the real heat-lovers.

Place the tray of seeds where it receives the most sunlight during the day. If you don't have a good place near a window, you can also germinate seeds under fluorescent lights; leave the lights on all the time, and raise the seedling trays on boxes so they are close to the light.

The moisture is held in the soil mix that you use. (It isn't literally soil, which would be too heavy for the tiny roots to penetrate. A more accurate term is *rooting medium*, but for simplicity let's call it *soil*.) The soil has to be sterile, has to be light, and has to hold water; a mix of peat moss, vermiculite, and perlite, in approximately equal proportions, works well. (See the chapter on Houseplants for more information on these ingredients.)

What container you use to hold this soil depends on how many seeds you are working with.

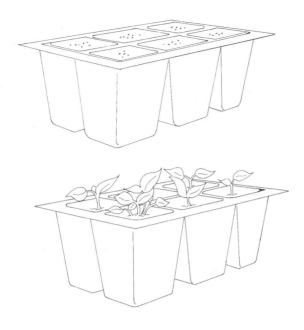

*Old six-packs, saved from last year, make terrific seed-starting containers.*

*Flats* are shallow containers with no interior dividers. You fill them with the soil, and then sow the seeds in rows. The main advantage of flats is that they conserve space; you can start many seeds in just one flat. The disadvantage is that there isn't room for the seedlings to grow vigorously if they stay in the flat, so you will have to transplant them to larger individual containers as an intermediate step. The drawing on this page illustrate the process.

You may find it simpler to start your seeds directly in separate containers, and let them grow to a size appropriate for transplanting into the garden. This eliminates the intermediate step, which is easier on you and on the baby plant.

The containers can come from a variety of sources. Many mail-order seed companies sell seed-starting apparatuses with everything you need. You can also be creative and recycle small plastic pots or six-packs from last year; if you didn't have a garden last year, your gardening buddies will be happy to share some of the millions of empty pots they have saved.

Once you start thinking in these terms, you will see many household items that you can use for seed starters. I like paper cups and carryout food containers, especially if they have removable clear plastic tops (makes a mini-greenhouse).

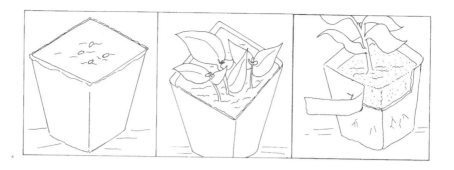

*Peat pots (either round or, as here, square) filled with sterile soil for starting seeds. After seeds sprout, prune down to strongest seedling. When ready to go into the ground, you plant the pot and its contents, minimizing transplant shock. Tear off the top of the pot, down to the soil line, before planting.*

Even simpler, use peat pots filled with your seedling soil mix. These pots, which come in round and square shapes and in several sizes, are made of compressed peat moss (see above). They go directly into the ground. You don't have to remove the seedling, because the roots grow right through the sides of the pot. Advantage: zero transplant shock.

Simplest of all are compressed pellets made of peat (see page 185). Flat when you buy them, they expand many times when wet. They are solid peat, so you do not need to fill them with your soil mix; just rehydrate, add seed, and when ready plant the whole thing in the ground.

All these containers should be set down inside a tray or shallow pan, to catch drips from watering.

Once the seedlings appear and start to grow, you must keep a careful eye on the soil moisture; the individual small pots will dry out quickly. Seedlings are also vulnerable to a fungus disease called damping off, which will kill them in a flash. One way to take care of both concerns is to water the containers with water in which you have mixed a fungicide specifically for damping off (check the label). Pour this water into the holding tray, and it will be drawn up into the soil of the individual pots.

It's a good idea to plant several seeds in each container, as a bit of insurance. If they all germinate, however, you should thin down to the strongest one. Use small scissors to snip off the extras right at the soil line; pulling them out could damage the roots of the one you want to keep.

If your timing is good, the seedlings will reach transplanting size at about the same time the weather is ready to receive them. You will have a much greater

*Peat pellets start out flat, about the size of silver dollars, and expand when wet. Seedling roots grow right through the peat, and the entire package is planted into the ground. Thin down to one strong seedling.*

chance of a successful move if you acclimate the seedlings gradually. The process is called "hardening off."

The first day, set the little plants outside for just an hour, then bring them back indoors. The second day, put them outside for two hours. The third day, four hours. The fourth day, six hours. And so on. By the end of a week, they are ready to be planted in the garden. At this point, the planting process is just like that described in the Container section of the Planting chapter.

SEEDS

**SHRUBS**

*I*n relative size and overall visual impact on the landscape, shrubs fill a middle spot between trees on one end and perennials and annuals at the other end. They grow more slowly than perennials, and can take five years or more to reach their full size. But their great advantage is that, once established, they don't need much fussing over.

There are three main categories of shrubs:

1. *Deciduous.* Like all deciduous plants, these shrubs lose their leaves in winter. Most of them flower, and many have stunning fall foliage. Examples: forsythia, hydrangea, viburnum.
2. *Broadleaf evergreen.* These shrubs have their foliage year-round, and usually showy flowers as well. By the way, *broadleaf* doesn't necessarily mean that the leaf is broad in size, only that it's not a needle or scale shape (see illustration on page 208). Examples: rhododendron, andromeda, boxwood.
3. *Conifers.* They don't all produce cones, but "conifer" is the best shorthand term for all the low- to medium-growing needle-leaf and scale-leaf plants used as shrubs. Examples: juniper, yew, arborvitae.

Shrubs come in a range of sizes; there are dwarf shrubs, low-growing shrubs that hug the ground, and larger species that will reach the height of small trees. Whether a particular plant is a large shrub or a small tree is sometimes a matter of debate. However, the fundamental difference is that unlike trees, which have one main stem (the trunk) that is bare until it branches partway up, shrubs have multiple stems and foliage all the way down to the ground. This creates a dense, full look that gardeners capitalize on, placing shrubs where they will fill in the "empty" space at the bottoms of trees or where they will screen out an unlovely sight.

# Designing with Shrubs

Making good design choices about shrubs depends on understanding some of their basic botanical characteristics. To repeat the most important:

- Shrubs grow slowly. If you space them properly, taking into account the size they will eventually reach, there will be lots of bare space for a few years. (Solution: fill the gaps with perennials, which are easy to move later.)
- Deciduous shrubs are bare in the winter. If you hoped to create a permanent screen, you'll be disappointed when you wake up one fall day and find all the leaves gone.
- They have strong, deep root systems and moving them is not what you would call a snap. Before planting choose the location *carefully*.
- Shrubs grow in certain general shapes and forms. Even when it is as big as it is going to get, a low, spreading shrub will still be low and spreading. Learn which varieties take which forms, and choose accordingly.

Basically, shrubs are used in two general ways in the landscape:

1. As a mass planting to create a screen or backdrop.
2. As individual accent plants.

Regrettably, we gardeners have overemphasized the first and underemphasized the second.

The dense growth that characterizes most shrubs has led to one of their most common uses in the landscape: foundation plantings—that is to say, shrubs planted tight up against the house. Originally the idea was to hide the foundation, when foundations were ugly, and to create a transition between the hard rectangle of the house and the (theoretically) soft contours of the yard. The habit persists, even though modern houses don't usually have eyesore foundations. Poor plant choices abound, which is why we see so many homes with huge overgrown shrubs obscuring the house and windows.

---

### Top 10 Foliage Shrubs

Some of these produce flowers, but they are not the primary characteristic of the plants.

*Sunny locations*
1. Euonymous
2. Golden spirea
3. Barberry (red or gold leaf varieties)
4. Variegated boxwood ("Oregonia")
5. Manzanita

*Shady locations*
6. Nandina
7. Aucuba
8. Oregon grape
9. Skimmia
10. Holly (shrub species)

---

Used thoughtfully, shrubs en masse can create a pleasing perimeter line or anchor the "heavy" end of a garden area. In woodland gardens, they produce the mid-layer between tall trees and very low plants. Banked along a fence or garage, they make a solid-green background against which to display bright flowers. And of course, massed in a tight line, shrubs of the same species become a hedge, described in its own chapter in this book.

Shrubs as accent plants deserve more attention. Here we are speaking of a single shrub, with some outstanding characteristic such as striking foliage or unusual winter bark, placed in a spot to take greatest advantage of that feature. That one shrub then becomes a focal point.

Accent shrubs can stand alone in the midst of a lawn, in grand and solitary splendor, or they can coexist graciously with other plants, such as in a mixed border. In the latter case, the finesse in designing is to surround the shrub with other plants that complement its best features. For example, late spring bulbs that pick up the shrub's unusual leaf color, or a mass of soft apple-green ground cover providing visual support for a shrub cascading with yellow flowers. Done well, this produces a garden where the whole is greater than the sum of the parts.

# Buying and Planting Shrubs

At the nursery, you will find shrub plants in three forms:

1. *Bareroot.* (Deciduous shrubs.)
2. *Containers.* (All kinds of shrubs.)
3. *Balled-and-burlapped (B&B).* (Evergreen shrubs.)

These three ways of packaging are described in the chapter on Planting, along with tips on choosing a good plant and step-by-step planting instructions.

| When to Plant Shrubs | |
| --- | --- |
| B&B | Spring or early fall. |
| Bareroot | When the plant is dormant: late fall, winter, or early spring. |
| Container | Any time the ground is not frozen, but early fall is ideal. |

If you should decide to move a shrub from one place to another in your yard, the best time to do it is in early spring, while the plant is still dormant.

# Caring for Your Shrubs

Your new shrubs need you most during their first year. In particular, keep an eye on water. Whenever it doesn't rain for a week, water them well. To conserve moisture, mulch all around the new shrub, but not right up to the base of the plant.

Add balanced fertilizer in the spring when new growth starts, and again after the plant has finished flowering.

Shrubs that produce lots of flowers look very scraggly unless they are faithfully deadheaded.

As winter approaches, water deeply and apply a thick layer of mulch, to keep the dormant plant from drying out.

Pruning established shrubs will promote vigorous new growth and help to maintain a pleasing shape. The common points of anxiety are where to cut and when to do it. Review the general principles and the illustrations in the Pruning chapter, and remember these common-sense fundamentals:

- Don't cut off flower buds. The shrubs that bloom in spring set their flower buds the year before; wait till they have finished blooming to prune. Summer-flowering shrubs produce flower buds that spring; so you can prune in winter, while plant is dormant, without harming buds.
- Pruning encourages new growth. Therefore you don't want to do it just before cold weather, or the new growth could freeze.

*I*n the garden, soil quality is everything. It is also boring, unglamorous, messy, and invisible. If your soil needs work to improve its quality (and every gardener since Adam and Eve has qualified), that work is also boring, messy, and unglamorous—and backbreaking to boot. It is also totally essential.

Good soil is "alive"—a mixture of minerals (in the form of minute particles of rocks), decayed organic material, air, water, and living organisms.

**SOIL**

## *Texture and Structure*

Soil texture is a function of the size of the individual particles within it. For several reasons, texture is the most critical facet of your soil; more on that in a moment.

*Soil structure* refers to the minuscule channels, tubes, and passageways that run through the soil, through which air and water pass. From our point of view as gardeners, it is important mostly as something that can be damaged by compaction. Continually walking over soil, or driving a car over it, will ruin its structure. So will, to a lesser degree, aggressively tilling it with a rototiller. There are times when rototilling is the only reasonable course, but you should realize that when you do it you are also disrupting soil texture. That is one reason why most gardeners (if they do it at all) rototill only once—when they first prepare a planting bed—not over and over every year. (The other reason is that it's hard work.)

Now to texture, and the main types of soil.

Sand   Sand particles are the largest.
In medium sand, one average particle is
$^1/_{50}$ of an inch in diameter. Sand
particles are squarish.

*A rototiller is sometimes necessary for breaking up neglected soil, digging up lawn, or preparing a new garden bed for the first time. Do not do this when the soil is very wet, or you will create serious compaction problems.*

Silt    Silt particles are the next in size. One particle is $1/500$ of an inch. They are relatively flat.

Clay    Clay particles are the smallest—$1/12{,}500$ of an inch. They are also flat.

Loam    Loam is the term for soil that has a mixture of all three types of particles.

Small, flat particles fit together more closely than large, square ones. This tiny fact, so obvious on its surface, is critically important to gardeners, and here's why:

As plants grow, they require both air and water. That seems self-evident, since all living things need air and water, but let's take just a minute to think about plants. Plants need air because:

1. They need to breathe.
2. The tiny root hairs that take in nutrients need room to grow, and air provides the open space that allows them to reach out.

Plants need water because:

1. It is a part of all cells.
2. Nutrients can be taken in by the roots only when they are dissolved in water.

Now, in all soils air and water are found in the open spaces between the soil particles. So the size of those spaces determines how much air and water are held in the soil.

Water, when it soaks into soil, adheres to the individual particles in a microscopically thin film. (It soaks into organic matter as into a sponge, which is one reason organic material is so important in soil; more on that in a moment.) The thinner a particle is, the greater its surface area in relation to its overall mass. And that is why clay soil, with its high proportion of those very thin particles, holds water longer than sandy soil. That is also why clay soils are called "heavy." This is not totally bad: it means that dissolved nutrients stay in the soil longer.

Sandy soil, by contrast, has comparatively large spaces between its particles. Water passes through it readily, carrying away the nutrients.

The size of the spaces is also important because of the interrelated effect on air.

Clay          Silt          Sand          Loam

*The four types of soil (left to right): Clay, with extremely tiny particles; silt; sand; and loam, which has some of all in a mixture.*

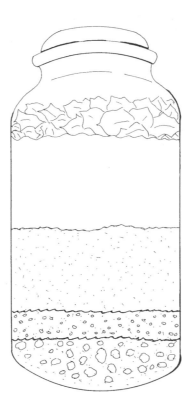

*A simple test to determine your soil content. A jar half full of garden soil is vigorously mixed with water and allowed to settle. The particles settle out in order of weight: sand, then silt, then clay, then the water, with organic matter floating on top. This sample is mostly clay.*

Clay and silty soil have comparatively less air space to begin with because of the size and shape of their particles. If those spaces are totally filled with water, the plants will die from suffocation.

You can see that there is a positive and negative side to both tiny air spaces and larger air spaces. That is why loam, with a mix of all kinds of particles, is such good soil for gardening. Another reason is that loam usually contains a fair amount of organic material, with all its benefits. Then you have what gardeners lovingly call "good garden loam," the stuff they swoon over.

> ### A Simple Drainage Test
> 1. Dig a hole one foot deep.
> 2. Fill it with water and let it drain out completely; that way the surrounding soil is saturated and capillary action won't distort the next step.
> 3. Immediately fill with water again and start timing.
> 4. Check the hole in two hours. If the water is all drained out, you're okay. If not, look again an hour later. If the hole is still half full of water, you have a problem.

### DRAINAGE

A related concern is how well, or how poorly, your soil drains. Obviously this has to do with whether it is clay or sand, but it also has to do with how deep your topsoil is and whether you have a hard impermeable sublayer.

Topsoil is the name that we give to the uppermost layer of soil where all the action is: where the air pores are, where the nutrients are found, where the organic material has settled, where the earthworms are at work, and so forth. If you or someone else has been gardening in that area, working the soil and adding conditioners, the topsoil will extend down as far as you have worked. If nothing has been done, the depth of topsoil is whatever it is—an accident of geology.

Below the topsoil is the subsoil; it will be sandy or silty or clayey, depending on your particular geology, but it will not be particularly fertile. Whatever organic material naturally fell to earth in eons past doesn't reach down that far, and so the soil worms and bacteria don't live there. Naturally, the subsoil drains well if it is solid sand, not at all if it is solid clay.

Between the two there may be a rock-hard layer of densely compacted earth known as a soil pan, or *hardpan*. It might have been put there by Mother Nature, or it might have been created when someone (not you, of course) foolishly rototilled when the soil was too wet. In either case, it will block water as effectively as if it were a layer of concrete (which, if it is dried, compacted clay, it resembles exactly).

So, no matter how beautiful your topsoil is, if you have a heavy subsoil, or a hardpan, or both, you have a drainage problem. If you intend to grow anything that has roots longer than your topsoil is deep, you will need to amend the soil, following the advice in this chapter. In severe cases, you may have to add some kind of mechanical drainage system, which is probably a job for a professional contractor.

Another characteristic of soil that has an effect on your garden is its pH. That stands for "potential Hydrogen," and it's written that way: lower-case p, upper-case H.

It is a numeric scale that measures how alkaline or acidic some substance is; the lower numbers are very acidic (lemon juice is 2), and higher numbers are very alkaline (baking soda is 8, ammonia is 11); 7 is neutral.

Why should we care about pH? For one thing, remember that plants take in nutrients only when they are dissolved in water. Some do not dissolve in very acidic or alkalinic media. For another, some plants have a definite pH preference; rhododendrons and azaleas, for instance, thrive only in acidic soils.

Most plants do well in soil that is neutral to slightly acidic, 6 to 7.

There is a relation between pH and rainfall. Where rainfall is high, forested ecosystems develop. As forest materials decay, acids are released, so soil that forms in these areas tends to be acidic. In the prairies of the midwestern United States, with moderate rainfall and resulting grasslands, there is more modest decomposition and hence soils have pH closer to neutral. In desert regions, with minimal rainfall and vegetation, soils are alkaline.

## TESTING PH

You can check soil pH yourself, with either a home test kit or a pH meter. Both can be purchased at a large garden center. For a more precise evaluation, you can have a full soil analysis done either at a commercial lab or your County Extension office, if they offer that service. It's more expensive, of course, but a full analysis will also tell you other things about your soil, including any mineral deficiencies.

It may seem that one number higher or lower wouldn't make much difference, but the pH scale is logarithmic; 4 is ten times more acidic than 5 and one hundred times more than 6. Changing the pH of a large area, by even one number, requires adding a huge amount of material. The wiser course for gardeners is to choose plants that match their existing conditions.

# Other Soil Terminology

You can see that there is a lot to know about soil. To make matters worse, some people have the frustrating habit of using other words when speaking of soil. Add a few of these to your vocabulary and casually toss them in when you're around more experienced gardeners.

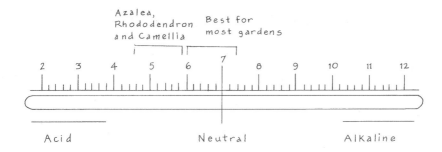

*The pH scale measures relative acidity of soil.*

- *Fertility* in relation to soil refers to its content of nutrients. Soil can be fertile naturally, because Mother Nature gifted it with a high level of nutrient-providing materials and the water to dissolve them, or because dedicated gardeners have stepped in.
- *Rich* soil has a high proportion of nutrients; *lean* is the opposite.
- *Friable* is not something you could cook with bacon for breakfast, but the term for a certain kind of texture. Soil is friable when it is dense enough to hold together when you squeeze a handful but loose enough to fall apart when you poke that handful. Friable is crumbly. Friable is good.
- *Sweet* means neutral or toward the alkaline end of the pH scale. Very acidic soil needs to be *sweetened*.
- *Tilth* is another name for texture. If soil is loose and friable, and rich with organic material, we say it "has good tilth."
- *Humus* is the name for organic material that is thoroughly decomposed; it is dark-colored, rich-looking, crumbly soil material. That is also how you would describe compost at the end of its decomposition cycle, but in practice people tend to use *humus* for what we find in nature and *compost* for the stuff we manufacture at home.

## Organic Content

Organic material is, by definition, something that was once alive, either plant or animal. All you have to do is take a walk in the woods to get a sense of it: pieces of plants, trees, mosses in varying stages of decay are all around you. Also there, but perhaps less visible, are animal remains. Within the soil, small worms, bacteria, and fungi are eating and digesting those plant and animal parts, and excreting protein-rich waste products. It is one enormous cycle of growth, decomposition, and new growth.

The soil in your garden was at one point rich in the decomposed material of its original ecosystem. But centuries of cultivation have changed the natural cycle, and now your soil has organic matter only if you purposefully add it.

Which I urge you to do. It is the single best thing you can do for your soil, and therefore your garden.

We have already encountered some of the benefits of organic material as a soil ingredient, but here's a summary:

• Absorbs and holds water like a sponge.
• Releases nutrients back into the soil as it decomposes.
• Improves the texture of all soils by adding particles of varying sizes.

The amazing thing is, organic material is the solution for soil that is too sandy, and also for soil that is too high in clay. In the first case, it changes the ability of the soil to hold water. In the second case, it introduces air spaces into the dense clay particles.

Sources of organic material include:

• Compost, either homemade or purchased.
• Dried leaves, pine needles, grass clippings, and the like.
• Straw and hay.
• Shredded newspaper.
• Weeds that you have pulled up (try not to include seed heads).
• Animal manure (well-rotted). Don't include droppings from housepets.
• Commercial mulch materials made from bark (bark chips, bark dust).
• Peat moss.

> Adding organic material has the effect of making the soil more acidic over time. Do a pH test every year.

Keeping a good level of organic material is an ongoing, never-ending process. (It decays, remember, and needs to be replenished.)

• Whenever you prepare a new bed for planting, work in some kind of organic material.
• When you're finished planting, pile on a mulch of organic materials, to conserve soil moisture and protect the plants against severe weather. Eventually, the mulch will break down into the soil, contributing more organic goodies; mulch anew.

- When you add new plants in later years, work some good organic stuff into the hole and also into the soil you took out of it, which you will use for backfill.

# Improving Your Soil

Unless the gods are smiling on you, you probably didn't start out with wonderful soil. All is not lost. There are steps you can take to correct every disadvantageous situation.

But first, for all the improvements that involve adding something to the soil, there's a right way and a wrong way to do it. The wrong way is simply to dump the new stuff on top of the soil, spread it around with a rake, and walk away. The right way is to thoroughly and completely incorporate it in, down to the level that you expect plant roots to grow. At the very least, one shovel depth. (That shovel-depth dimension, incidentally, is called a *spit*, if you really want to impress your new gardening cohorts.)

The process goes by the shorthand phrase of "work the soil" or "work the [whatever] in." It requires a shovel, a garden fork, your hands, and your back.

### ADDING AMENDMENTS TO YOUR SOIL

1. Digging down with the shovel one spit deep (isn't that fun to say?), remove and set aside one chunk of soil; that gives you room to work.
2. Now pour in your amendment of choice until the hole is half full. Using the fork, pull in some adjacent soil and mix it around and around, lifting and turning, until it is well integrated.
3. Dig another hole, and keep going. If you create or uncover any large clods of soil, break them up with the fork or your hands.
4. As much as possible, avoid standing on the section you have already worked.
5. At the end, incorporate some amendment into the pile you set aside, and add it back to the bed.

If your soil is extremely poor, or if you intend to plant things with a deep root system such as trees or large shrubs, you may need to do what is known as (and spoken of in tones of dread) double digging.

### DOUBLE DIGGING

Basically, double digging means digging down the depth of two shovel blades, or twice as deep as single digging. It is bloody hard work, but here's how to do it if you insist.

1. Mentally divide the area you're working on into smaller sections: either squares or narrow strips, depending on overall size of the bed. In the first section, dig a hole or trench down to the depth of one shovel blade. Set that soil aside on a wide board or plastic cloth.
2. In that same hole or trench, dig and loosen the second layer, below what you just removed, with a garden fork. Work in some soil amendment. You now have an empty trench with a loose, crumbly sublayer.
3. Move over to the next adjacent section. With the fork, work in soil amendment to the top layer and then shovel that improved soil into the first trench, filling in the empty spot.
4. Dig down to the second layer of the second trench; fluff it up with the fork and work in amendents.
5. Continue this pattern until you reach the end of the area you intend to improve. Fill in the very last trench with the soil you removed from the first one.

## TO IMPROVE TEXTURE OF CLAY SOIL

### ADD SAND

When it is thoroughly incorporated into very clayey soil, sand, with its larger particles, has the effect of forcing the smaller clay particles apart and introducing air spaces into the soil. The difficulty is, it takes a lot of sand to gain an appreciable result: 1 inch of sand for every 3 inches of soil. That works out to 9 cubic yards per 1,000 square feet of garden space, and that's a lot of sand. Sand is very heavy, and wrestling that amount into position is a killer. To do an entire bed, a small rototiller (see illustration on page 192) comes in handy.

The better way to use sand is to incorporate it into individual planting holes for specific plants that insist on well-drained soil, such as lilies. In a small area like that, you can manage the weight and bulk of the sand.

Just make sure you get coarse sand; fine sand won't help your problem at all. You want river sand, not beach sand; salt is harmful to plants. You can buy river sand in bags in the garden center, or at building supply stores for a fraction of the cost (it's what contractors use to make concrete).

### ADD ORGANIC MATERIAL

For all the reasons described above, organic matter greatly improves soil texture. Depending on how high your clay content is, you should aim for an amount of organic matter that is one-half to one-quarter the volume of the soil you are working on.

When adding organic matter that is high in carbon and low in nitrogen (sawdust, wood shavings, bark chips, straw), mix in some pure nitrogen fertilizer, especially if the material is fresh, not at all decomposed. The wonderful little microorganisms in the soil that do all the work need nitrogen for food, and if they do not find it in the organic stuff you add, they will take it directly from the soil, robbing it from plant roots.

## IMPROVING TEXTURE OF SANDY SOIL

You would think that if you add sand to clay soil to improve its texture, the reverse process should work for sandy soil. But to tell you the truth, I've never heard of adding clay—and I wouldn't know where to tell you to get it. One compromise approach is to work in an equal measure of garden loam or good topsoil, purchased at a large garden supply outlet. Then what you will have is "sandy loam," which is less than pure loam but better than what you started with.

The better course is to add organic material—exactly as you would with clay soil.

# Improving Drainage

You never have a drainage problem with sandy soil, unless it is sitting on top of hardpan just a few inches down. Drainage difficulties go hand in hand with clay soils.

If you have already taken measures to improve the texture of your soil and the drainage problem persists, that means you have a very shallow topsoil or a hardpan or both. The solutions are:

- Loosen the subsoil with double digging (see page 199)—very hard work.
- Break up the hardpan with some long, sharp digging tool—very, very hard work.
- Bring in topsoil and compost and build a raised bed (see page 156). Gets my vote every time.
- Go with the flow—plan a bog garden, with water-loving plants.

If you are starting out fresh with a brand-new garden, one that has never been planted, and have a severe drainage problem, it will probably be worth it to hire a professional to build in a drainage bed or pipes. In my opinion, it is seldom worth the expense in established gardens where you simply wish to add a new border or bed.

# Changing pH

Remember, low numbers are acidic, higher numbers are alkaline. Raising pH is increasing alkalinity; lowering it is increasing acidity.

### MAKING SOIL LESS ACIDIC

To raise the pH of soil, making it more alkaline, add lime in some form.

- Packaged lime from the garden center. The most common kind, called "dolomite lime," is lime (calcium carbonate) plus magnesium carbonate (magnesium is an important secondary nutrient). It may be labeled "agricultural lime." Hydrated lime (also called quicklime or slaked lime) is produced when water is added to calcium oxide. This is the stuff used to make whitewash, and is not recommended for garden use.
- Organic sources include crushed eggshells, finely ground shells of shellfish like oysters or clams, and bonemeal. Bonemeal is considered a fertilizer, but it also has the effect of raising pH. These organic forms work more slowly.
- Wood ashes also raise pH; they contain calcium carbonate, along with potassium, phosphorus, and trace minerals. Scatter lightly over your garden every two years.

*How Much?* To raise pH by one unit, you need between 5 and 10 pounds of lime per 100 square feet of garden space (sandy soils need less, clay soils more). Best time to apply is fall; winter rains will help break it down. Weather conditions will gradually wipe away the added lime; after three or four years, you'll need to add some more.

Your very best approach: Get a soil test and follow the recommendations that come with the results.

### MAKING SOIL MORE ACIDIC

To lower the pH of soil, and thus make it less alkaline, add sulfur in one of these mineral forms.

- Ammonium sulfate or aluminum sulfate. (The latter is faster acting, but don't use it around vegetables.)
- Gypsum (which also contains calcium).
- Iron sulfate (which also contains iron).

*How much?* The various forms of sulfur have different application rates; pay attention to package directions.

As a rule of thumb, to adjust soil that is now 7.5 to approximately 6.5 for the following types of soil:

- Sandy loam, apply 1½ pounds per 100 square feet.
- Loam soil, 2 pounds per 100 square feet.
- Clay soil, 2½ pounds per 100 square feet.

Various organic materials, normally added for their overall benefits to soil, also have the effect of lowering pH:

Peat moss.

Tea leaves and coffee grounds.

Oak leaves and pine needles.

Cottonseed meal, bloodmeal, and urea—organic forms of fertilizer—also make soil more acidic.

**TOOLS**

*a* good tool is a wondrous thing, and the right tools make gardening chores much simpler. But there's no reason to go overboard. Don't forget, men and women gardened for millenia with nothing but a pointed stick.

The following are what I consider really basic:

- Trowel
- Shovel
- Garden fork
- Rake
- Small clippers

With those five, you can: dig a hole of any size, work in soil amendments, and rake the area smooth. With the edge of a rake or the tip end of the handle you can draw rows for planting seeds. And when things start to grow madly, you can keep them trimmed with the clippers.

> ### Tip: Bright Handles
>
> Tools with plain green or dirt-colored handles are hard to see if you lay them down among the plants. Spray the handles with bright fluorescent paint.

If your plans or your personality call for it, you can add these others:

- Small hand cultivator, for loosening soil and weeding close to plants.
- Leaf rake (you can use the garden rake for leaves, but a true leaf rake is much easier).
- A small weeding tool (when you get tired of yanking things up by hand).
- Hoe, handy for chopping weeds and general cultivation.
- Big loppers, for branches and stems too thick for your hand clippers. (Illustrated on page 154.)
- Hedge shears, pretty essential if you have a hedge. (Illustrated on page 154.)

*Terrific tools, left to right: Hand pruners, weed digger, leaf rake, shovel, garden fork, hoe, garden rake, trowel, small fork/cultivator.*

Buy the best quality you can afford. In the long run, it's cheaper.

And once you have good tools, take care of them. Keep them clean (well, reasonably so) all during the season. If you put your garden to bed in the winter, clean, oil, and store your tools too. Whatever has a sharp edge, keep it sharp. If you don't know your way around a sharpening stone, find someone who sharpens scissors for a living to do this for you. Make it a practice to do this once a year.

## Gloves Are Tools Too

When it comes to gloves, gardeners tend to fall into two camps: There are buy-only-the-best-so-they-will-last folks and the buy-the-cheapest-because-they-just-get-dirty folks. I confess I tend to fall in the second camp. I buy inexpensive cotton gardening gloves by the fistful when they're marked down; I wear them until they fall apart or get so encrusted with mud they're stiff as cardboard, and then throw them away. Over the years I don't think I've spent any more on them than those folks who insist on only the finest leather. Maybe less.

> ## Tip: Gloves
>
> Gloves protect your hands from sharp thorns, blisters, and the accidental encounter with giant slugs. But if all you want to do is keep your hands dry and mud-free when it's raining, try surgical gloves from the pharmacy. They're thin enough to provide good dexterity, but thick enough to keep your fingernails from poking through.

*T*rees in the garden are like the major bones in your body: they form the basic structure and support the smaller elements like shrubs and flowers. But that is only the beginning. Trees also give us shade and buffer us from wind. They absorb intrusive noise and block out unattractive vistas. With their beautiful foliage, flowers, and bark, they brighten the landscape. They sing in the wind and glisten in the rain. And they do all this while asking little from us in return.

You do have to do your homework when choosing which trees to plant. And young trees will benefit from intelligent pruning and fertilizing. But once established, most trees need only minimal attention from gardeners.

---

### Top 10 Small to Medium Trees

1. Dogwood
2. Sourwood
3. Crabapple
4. Japanese snow bell
5. Flowering plum
6. Harlequin glory bower (*Clerodendrum*)
7. Vine maple
8. Japanese maple
9. Honey locust
10. Golden chain (*Laburnum*)

---

## Tree Basics

Before deciding which trees to include in your garden plan, and where, it is necessary to learn one fundamental fact about trees: the difference between deciduous and evergreen.

- *Deciduous* trees lose their leaves in the fall, when the days get short and the temperature cools.
- *Evergreen* trees have foliage in place all year long. Not that leaves (or needles) are permanent; they continu-

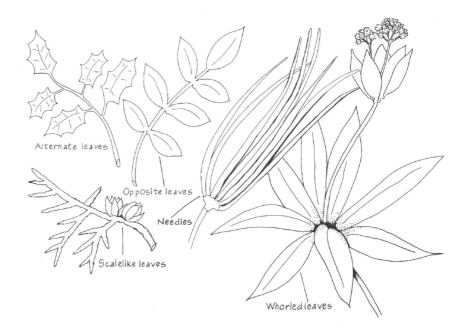

*The type of leaf structure is one important part of plant identification. It also contributes to overall texture of trees and all other plants.*

ally die off and are replaced by new ones, but the tree is never without foliage.

Evergreen trees are further categorized by their foliage. They may have broad, flat leaves, needles, or scales. Broadleaf evergreen trees are in the minority; examples are magnolia and Pacific madrone. Needle-leaf trees are the most common; think of pines, spruces, firs. Some evergreen trees have what is known as scalelike foliage: junipers and cedars, for instance.

Most evergreen trees are *conifers*, meaning that they produce cones; sometimes the two terms are used interchangeably.

And just to keep us on our toes, there are some surprises. Larches, for example, are conifers with needle-leaf foliage—and they are deciduous.

The distinction between the two major types is important for both esthetic and practical reasons.

You must choose deciduous trees if you want:

- The hot splash of fall color.
- The dramatic look of bare branches in a winter landscape.

- Flowers (with a few exceptions).
- Sunlight through the limbs in winter, shade in summer.

You must choose evergreen trees if you want:

- A permanent, dense mass, as a screen or backdrop.
- Shade all year long.

# Designing with Trees

The choice of deciduous versus evergreen is only the first of many decisions you will have to make when selecting trees for your garden. Trees, like all other living parts of your landscape, have color, texture, shape, and mass.

Trees come in an array of shapes: pyramidal, columnar, vase, rounded, spreading, and weeping. (See illustration on page 52.) And many species have varieties representing a range of sizes and silhouettes: there are dwarf pyramids, creeping forms of upright trees, small and tall versions of practically everything. There is a spruce tree that gets to be 100 feet tall, and there is one called bird's-nest that is round, concave like a nest, and about 1 foot high. I'm sorry to say this, but there is such diversity in tree species, you really do have to research the specifics of the varieties you're interested in.

| Fast-Growing Trees |
| --- |
| 1. Willows |
| 2. Tree of heaven |
| 3. Golden chain (*Laburnum*) |
| 4. Tulip tree (*Liriodendron tulipifera*) |
| 5. Mimosa |
| 6. Mountain ash |

Not knowing the mature size of a tree can get you in serious trouble. Whenever you see a poor misshapen tree growing too close to a house, banging into the roof, you can bet it's because whoever planted it did not think about how big it would eventually get. Tall trees make large shade—maybe more than you want.

In addition to size, trees also have visual mass and texture. Some 20-foot trees are thick, heavy, blocky; other 20-foot trees are light, delicate, airy. Look at as many trees as you can: in your neighborhood, in arboretums, in books and magazines.

And then there is color.

In trees, color comes in strong doses from flowers and autumn foliage. It comes more subtly in the color of bark, berries or other fruit, in variegated leaves, and in the many splendid shades of green. (See the chapter on Color.) Looking at lots of trees is the best, the only way to find your personal favorites.

---

### Flowering Fruit Trees

Varieties of fruit trees that produce flowers but no fruit are called "ornamental." There are ornamental cherries, plums, crabapples, etc. Whether the absence of fruit is a plus or a minus is up to you; just be aware of what you are getting when the tree is called an "ornamental."

---

## Buying a Tree

Young trees come packaged in three ways:

1. Bareroot.
2. Balled-and-burlapped (B&B).
3. Containers.

These three types are described in the chapter on Planting, along with suggestions on how to choose healthy plants in these forms. That same chapter also describes the process of planting in each case. The procedures for trees is no different, except in one respect: stakes.

The purpose of a stake is to help the tree settle into a stable position, to protect it against the force of strong wind that could unseat it in the first months before the roots are fully developed.

The stake should be close to the trunk, no more than 6 inches away, and should extend up past the bottom branches. You can use one stake or two. Fasten the tree to the stake with a light rope, plastic cord, or a length of fabric. Leave some slack; you want the trunk to move with the wind, to develop its own flexibility. Remove stake after one year.

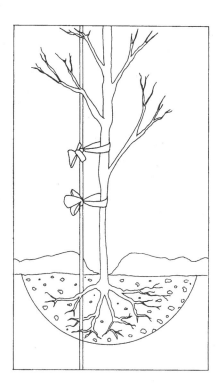

*Young bareroot tree planted, mulched, and staked.*

### When to Plant Trees

| | |
|---|---|
| Bareroot | When dormant; early spring is ideal. |
| Container | Anytime ground is not frozen; fall is ideal, lets roots get established before growth begins. |
| B&B | Early spring or early fall. |

## Caring for Your Tree

It is in the first year that your new tree needs the most attention.

- Fertilize three times: spring, summer, and fall.
- Water often; be especially alert during dry summer months.
- Keep the mulch thick; replace it as it disintegrates.

After the first year, your chores become easier.

- Fertilize once a year, in the spring.
- Water only if weather is unusually dry.
- Prune lower branches if they're in the way, otherwise prune only to correct problems. (See illustration on page 153.)

## Pruning and Moving

Trees can be pruned almost anytime, although when they are dormant is ideal, especially at the end of the dormant period: late winter. If the tree's flowers are your primary interest, wait to prune until after flowering has finished.

Moving a tree is a very hard job. Unless it is quite small, I recommend you call in a pro.

---

### Pruning Disasters

A tree has a natural, built-in urge to achieve a certain shape. If we interfere with that urge, the results are almost always hideous. The worst sin is cutting off the top (called topping), to make the tree shorter so it will fit in a smaller space. The tree is not going to pay any attention; in just a few years it will try to replace the amputated top with another, only it will be lopsided and goofy looking. It's not the tree's fault that it was planted in the wrong place.

---

Growing your own vegetables is enormously rewarding. Nothing beats the taste of a vine-ripened tomato, and nothing beats the joy of find ing fresh lettuce for tonight's salad right outside your kitchen door. Also, if you grew it yourself you know for a fact what chemicals were or were not used on it.

Unfortunately, growing them is not the easiest task in gardening. Vegetable plants are very attractive to a wide range of damaging insects. And, as every gardener since Nebuchadnezzar has known, persnickety weather can ruin your crop and then all your hard work is wasted. Still, remembering what supermarket tomatoes taste like, we persist.

The first thing to understand about vegetables is that, with a very few exceptions, they are annuals. They will die at the end of this year's growing season. So you must give them enough growing time to produce their produce before cold weather sets in. In many parts of the country, that means starting seeds indoors to get a jump on the weather (see Seed chapter for details). Much easier is buying small plants from someone else who started seeds indoors early— someone like a commercial grower. It also means you need to learn a few ways to trick Mother Nature into thinking it's warmer or colder than it actually is.

The second thing is that some of our popular vegetables grow very well in coolish weather and very poorly in hot weather; others are just the reverse. So timing is important.

## Planning Your Vegetable Garden

This is fair warning: looking through seed catalogs is very seductive. If you aren't careful, you will find yourself with way more varieties than you can realistically handle.

Start by deciding what you and your family really like to eat. Leave room to try something brand-new each season, but at the same time be honest: if no one likes turnips now, they're not suddenly going to develop a fondness for them just because you grew them.

Then, take note of the space requirements of the items on your working list. Melons, winter squashes, pumpkins, and corn, for example, take up huge amounts of space in relation to the goodies you get from them. If your only experience with cabbage is what you see in the supermarket, you'll be surprised how big the full plant is when it's growing in the ground. Same with Brussels sprouts.

Next, compare your tentative list against your growing season. If you live in the mountains, with a short growing season, and you have your heart set on watermelons, you're going to be disappointed. Seed catalogs are an excellent reference; they usually list "days to maturity" for all the varieties they sell.

## Cool-Season Vegetables

Peas
Beets
Radishes
Lettuce and other salad greens
Spinach
Cabbage and other family members:
    kale, Brussels sprouts, broccoli, kohlrabi
Onions (scallions)
Celery
Swiss chard

## Warm-Season Vegetables

Beans
Carrots
Tomatoes
Eggplant
Peppers
Squashes and Melons
Cucumbers
Potatoes
Lima beans (need hot weather)
Okra (needs really hot weather)

Finally, narrow your list even further by asking yourself which types and varieties you want to devote your garden space to, and which ones you can easily obtain elsewhere. For example, I do not grow carrots because they're available in the market year-round at very reasonable prices, and they're very hard to grow in the dense clay soil I have to cope with. But I always grow sugar snap peas because they're awesomely delicious and they haven't yet become staples in supermarket produce sections. Using that same logic, you might decide to grow unusual varieties of common vegetables (blue potatoes or yellow bell peppers) or gourmet vegetables and salad greens (arugula is no more trouble than ordinary lettuce)—things you cannot easily find at the regular market, at least not without paying a pretty penny.

---

### Top 10 Vegetables

1. Sweet 100 Tomatoes. A red cherry tomato that produces large sprays of incredibly sweet tomatoes.
2. Yellow pear tomatoes. A bright yellow, pear-shaped cherry tomato. It looks fabulous in salads.
3. Sugar snap peas. An outstanding achievement of vegetable breeders: edible pod pea with fat peas inside; crunchy and unbelievably sweet. Chosen the all-time vegetable winner by All-America Selection (see page 113).
4. Blue Lake snap beans. Wonderful old-fashioned flavor.
5. Packman broccoli. Cut off the top head, and new ones branch out from the sides.
6. Swiss chard. Holds well through cold weather, so you can have fresh greens up until very hard freeze.
7. Marketmore cucumbers. Actually, any homegrown cucumber is wonderful, I just happen to like this one.
8. Oakleaf or romaine lettuce. These two are pretty and foolproof.
9. Sunburst pattypan squash. This is one of those cute little round squashes with scalloped edges. Harvest when very small and bake or steam them whole.
10. Yukon Gold potatoes. Flesh is yellow, smooth textured, and has a rich buttery flavor.

---

## A Good Site

Vegetables need sun and lots of it—a minimum of 6 hours a day. This is especially true of all those that first produce a flower before the vegetable—tomatoes, beans, peas, cucumbers, squash, peppers, etc. You may be able to cheat a bit on leafy vegetables, but even they do better in a spot that gets full sun.

The soil must be rich and very loose. Many vegetable plants (but not tomatoes) have shallow root systems, so you can get away with working the soil down only about 10 inches, but do it thoroughly. And add *lots* of organic matter; getting water and nutrients to the roots is key to successful vegetables.

If you have several possible locations to choose from, all with good sun and good rich soil, pick the one that is closest to a water source. Vegetables need a lot of watering, and dragging hoses around is a bore.

## Growing Good Vegetables

Cool-season plants can be started in early spring, so that they are actively growing while the weather is still on the cool side. Most will reach maturity in late spring (in the South) or early summer (elsewhere). Really hot temperatures cause them to cease production (peas) or bolt (the leaf crops). Peas, beets, and radishes do better if they are direct seeded; everything else can be started as transplants.

Warm-season plants simply will not grow unless both the soil and the air have warmed up. Wait until night temperatures are 50 to 55 degrees before you plant either seeds or transplants.

You can take advantage of this seasonality by staging several types of vegetables in the same garden plot. It's called *interplanting,* and it's an excellent way to get double or triple use from your space. For example: In spring, put in baby lettuce plants and broccoli plants close together; the lettuce will be ready to harvest before the broccoli, and removing it opens up more growing space for the larger broccoli plants. After the lettuce is gone, and the broccoli is still producing, plant some bush bean seeds in among the broccoli. Once the broccoli has passed its peak and is ready to be pulled out, the beans will be up and flowering. Toward the middle of August, when the beans are being harvested, put in some Swiss chard transplants, and they'll flourish up through Thanksgiving. All in one compact garden space.

> The key to successful vegetables is to remember that they are heavy feeders. Give them lots of water and nutrient-rich soil. And once they start producing, harvest them frequently.

Once vegetables start to produce, you must keep them harvested. Even if you can't bear the thought of eating another zucchini this week, harvest them anyway. Remember that, as an annual, what this plant really wants to do is make seed and reproduce itself. Once a vegetable (which is the plant's seed incubator) is formed and stays on the plant long enough for the seeds to ripen into maturity, the plant will shut down—and no more vegetables.

### Vegetables: A Few Surprises

1. Mizuna. This Oriental salad green has very frilly leaves arranged in a large rosette shape.
2. Kohlrabi. A member of the cabbage family, this looks like a green or purple softball growing aboveground, with a few broccoli-like leaves arching up from the sides. The softball is the part you eat; it's crunchy like a turnip but sweeter. Great raw with dips.
3. Burgundy beans. Worth growing just for the color. These snap beans are a deep burgundy color when you pick them but turn green when you cook them.
4. Scarlet runner beans. Your grandmother remembers these: pole beans with rich orange flowers. Some people grow them just for the colorful flowers.
5. Chocolate Beauty bell peppers (chocolate color, not taste).

### GROW IN RAISED BEDS

Raised beds are ideal for vegetables. They allow you to provide the right amount of good, rich soil; they make for better drainage; and they create small, defined areas in which it is easier to monitor and control insects. Because you don't need paths between individual rows, as you would in traditional row planting, you get much more efficient use from your space.

Another advantage: raised beds also are a few degrees warmer than the level ground, and for vegetables that little bit can make all the difference. Covered with floating row covers, raised beds are even warmer.

Floating row covers are thin, porous strips of very lightweight fabric placed over the tops of vegetable plants while they are still small. You bury the edges but leave lots of slack on top; as the plants grow, they push the cover upward, so that it seems to float. The covers are primarily to keep out flying insects (such as cabbage moths that produce larvae that eat everything in sight), and they do it well; they also raise the temperature of the bed, like a quilt.

### GROW VERTICALLY

A number of your favorite vegetables grow on vines: cucumbers, beans, peas, melons, squashes. Try to grow them on some kind of vertical support: a fence already in place, a temporary short section of fence you install just for the vegetables, a trellis (but make it strong), or a strong wire or pole between two posts.

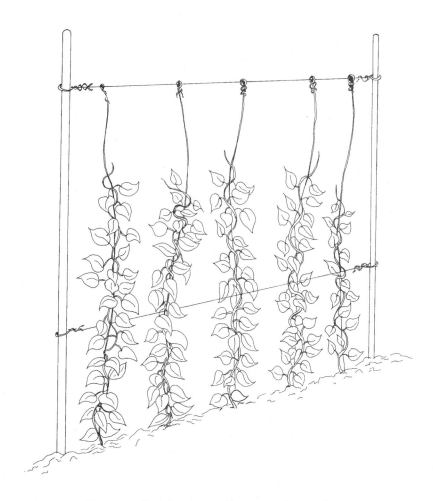

*By growing vegetables vertically (these beans illustrate only one of many techniques), you get a lot from a little ground space.*

Growing vegetables vertically has several advantages:

- You get much more efficient use of your space.
- Because they hang down instead of being scrunched against the soil, you get nice, straight vegetables.
- You're much less likely to step on them.

You may think you don't have room for an honest-to-God vegetable garden, or the time, but that doesn't mean you can't enjoy the pleasures of fresh vegetables. Just tuck individual plants in among your flower beds. Many vegetable plants are quite decorative. Here are a few examples; once you begin looking through seed catalogs with this idea in mind, you'll find many other candidates.

- New Zealand spinach is a low-growing, spreading plant with fleshy, edible leaves. It makes a handsome ground cover, and doesn't bolt in hot weather like true spinach does.
- Swiss chard and red Swiss chard are both very handsome upright plants.
- "Super pepper" is a small, tidy pepper plant that produces loads of very small and *very* hot chile peppers that sit up above the foliage in sassy flashes of red. In fact any of the peppers, both sweet and hot, would make an attractive addition to a sunny flower bed.

# Luscious Tomatoes and Other Specific Tips

**Tomatoes.** Plant them very deeply, much deeper than they were in their original container (see page 220). If you have a short growing season, select cherry tomatoes and other small varieties. Water deeply about once a week. Pinch off leafy branches that grow in the notches; prune away about half of the foliage. Stake the plants or grow them in tomato cages.

**Potatoes.** There are lots of intriguing new varieties, fun to grow and to eat. Plant "seed" potatoes (a chunk of a specially grown potato) in an 8-inch hole, fill halfway with soil; as green foliage grows through, keep adding more soil. Little potatoes form all along the underground stem. To avoid reinfecting with soil-borne diseases that persist through the winter, don't plant potatoes in the same spot two years in a row.

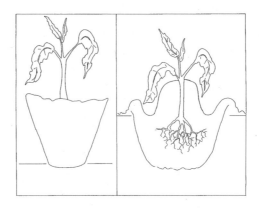

*Tomatoes need a lot of water and make deep roots. Help this one get off to a strong start by burying the full length of the stem; side roots will develop all along it.*

*You get more tomatoes in proportion to leaves if you pinch out stems that form in the notches. Prune off top for a more compact plant.*

**Lettuce and spinach.** Both are cool season crops and rather small plants, can sometimes be coaxed through hot weather if you plant them in the shade of a bean trellis (see page 221).

**Squash and cucumbers.** In bush form (rather than vining) they take up less space; one zucchini bush will give you more than enough for your family.

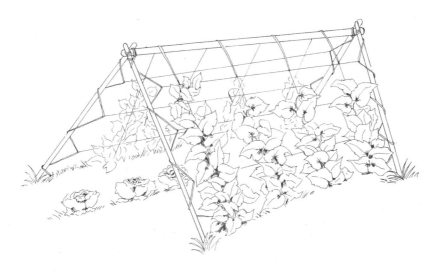

*These lettuces (a cool-season plant) grow reasonably happily in the shade of the bean trellis—at least better than they would in full summer sun.*

**Radishes**. These vegetables germinate extremely quickly. Intermix their seeds with seeds of slow germinators (like carrots or beets) to mark the spot and break up the soil surface.

**Lettuce**. In most home gardens, you'll have better luck with looseleaf lettuce rather than the kind that makes a tight head—or, more often, doesn't. Harvest just a few outside leaves and leave the plant in the ground to keep growing.

## Vegetables in Containers

It is possible to grow a surprising number of vegetables in containers, so even if you don't have a garden you can still enjoy sweet tomatoes and luscious lettuce. The trick is to find varieties bred to stay small. There is, for instance, a type of Japanese eggplant called "Little Fingers"; each eggplant is about 4 inches long and an inch in diameter. Study the seed catalogs; some of them suggest varieties for containers. Recognizing that people love homegrown tomatoes more than anything, breeders have developed a number of varieties for container growing. Look for names like

"Patio" or anything that suggests small size, such as "Tiny Tim." Cherry tomatoes can even be grown in a hanging container, with the stems dangling down.

Also, think of the vegetables that by their very nature are small plants: lettuce, onions, Swiss chard, carrots, radishes, beets, for example. All of them could easily be grown in a container.

Review the Container chapter for general information about gardening in this way. Remember that containers tend to dry out very fast. Coupled with the fact that most vegetables need lots of water, this means that you will have to watch the soil moisture like a hawk. When the weather is hot, dry, and windy, you may need to water vegetable containers several times a day.

*M*ake room in your garden for vines, for their charms are many:

- They contribute a vertical dimension.
- They block out unattractive views and provide a privacy screen.
- They cover up things you'd just as soon not look at, like the compost bin or the fence that's due for renovation someday.
- They provide shade for sunny spots.
- They attract bees, birds, and butterflies to your garden.

To add a vine to your garden plan, you need to be aware of two things: (1) whether the plant is annual or perennial, and (2) how it climbs.

The plants we call vines have three different mechanisms for attaching themselves to their support. Your job is to give them the type of support that matches their climbing method.

1. *Tendrils.* Thin "fingers" attached to the stem reach out and grab onto whatever is nearest, and then wind themselves very tightly around. They prefer something very skinny, such as a string trellis or a wire fence. Peas and sweet peas are examples of this type.
2. *Flexible stems.* These twining vines actually wind the entire stem—leaves, flowers, and all—around the support. To get dense coverage, give them a thick support such as a heavy pole or wide wooden trellis. Pole beans and wisteria are in this category.
3. *Hold-fasts.* Vines in this group have a kind of specialized structure that grabs onto flat supports. Some are short, flat roots (ivy is an example); others are like little suction cups (Virginia creeper). They grow best against a rough-surfaced wall or solid fence.
4. *Climbers.* These don't actually climb on their own but we call them "climbers" because their long, flexible branches look best attached to some kind of structure.

The plant has no way to attach itself, however, and depends on us to tie it in place. Bougainvillea and climbing roses are examples.

*Vines grow in four ways. Our job is to give them the kind of support they need. Tendrils (top left) wind tightly around very narrow supports like string. Twining plants (top right) wind the entire stem around a support; the fatter the support pole is, the tighter coverage you get. Vines with small roots (bottom left) attach themselves to a rough flat surface like this brick wall. Those in the fourth group don't vine at all, but need us to tie them to something.*

# Annual Vines

1. Sweet peas (tendrils). Easy to grow from seed, plant early in spring; lovely colors and intoxicating fragrance. Like other peas, grow strongly in late spring and fade in summer heat.
2. Blackeyed Susan vine (twining). Golden yellow flowers with large black "eye." Likes full sun, not fussy about soil. Plant seed after danger of frost has passed; showiest in late summer, early fall.
3. Scarlet runner beans (twining). Plant in sunny location after last spring frost. Grows fast, produces red/orange flowers that attract hummingbirds. An edible plant: huge bean pods with large purple and cream-colored beans. Dry them for soup in winter.
4. Morning glory (twining). Beautiful trumpet-shaped flowers in white, blue, pink, and red open in the morning, close in afternoon. Plant in eastern exposure after frost danger has passed; soak seeds overnight first. (*Note*: Wild morning glory, known as bindweed, is a horribly invasive pest. That's not what we're talking about here.)
5. Cardinal climber (Cypress vine) (twining). Plant seed in full sun after frost danger is past. Pretty leaves and small, bright red flowers are a favorite of hummingbirds. Slow to get started, but grows very fast in late summer heat, lasts well until frost.
6. Nasturtium (twining). There are several varieties; some are true climbers, others semi-vining. Very easy to grow. Bright flowers in shades of yellow/orange/red, and round leaves like miniature water lilies. Flowers are edible, as long as you don't use toxic chemicals in your soil preparation or maintenance.

# Perennial Vines

1. Clematis (loosely twining, appreciates some help). Many varieties, for spring, summer, and fall bloom. Flowers in a wide range of colors, all spectacular. Needs a permanent and very sturdy trellis.
2. Ivy (hold-fasts). Lots of varieties, some with variegated foliage. To preserve your sanity in later years, choose a noninvasive type.
3. Honeysuckle (twining, with some help). Popular woody deciduous vine with several good varieties. Fragrant flowers in pink, cream, yellow/orange, red/yellow. Hummingbirds consider them ambrosia. Needs occasional hard pruning to keep in control, otherwise relatively carefree.

4. Climbing hydrangea (hold-fasts). Flowers are the lace-cap type, cream colored. A hardy deciduous vine that forms a beautiful pattern against a wall even after leaves fall.

5. Star jasmine (twining, but needs help). Woody, evergreen vine that flowers from late spring till frost. Not a true jasmine but has the same exquisite fragrance. Needs protection in severe winters, otherwise hardy.

6. Rose (climber, train by hand). The queen of climbing plants: all colors of flowers, most very fragrant. Choose location carefully. Some climbing roses can get to be 100 years old, and need a very strong structure on which to grow.

**P**lants need water so their cells stay firm and the plant doesn't flop over. They also need water because the nutrients, which are in the soil, can be taken in by the roots only when they are dissolved in water.

The tricky part about watering is knowing when to do it and how much to give. I am very sorry to have to tell you this, but there is no good rule of thumb. The rate at which soils and plants lose water is affected by many things: air temperature, soil temperature, wind, amount and intensity of sunshine, type and texture of soil, size and shape of leaf, overall size of plant, and Mother Nature's whim. The best thing you can do is learn some general guidelines, and start building your own sensibilities about your garden by accumulated observation.

## General Guidelines About Water and Watering

1. Water moves downward; it does not, except to a minor degree, move sideways.
2. Clay particles hold water tightly, like a magnet. So do particles of organic matter, which absorb it like a sponge.
3. Too much water is as harmful to plants as too little. It fills in all the pores in the soil, driving out air.
4. To do a plant any good, water must reach its roots. So deep watering less frequently is more useful than shallow watering more often.
5. Garden plants need water in the soil, not in the air around them (one exception: houseplants that require high humidity). Oscillating sprinklers that lose most of their water to evaporation are wasteful.
6. The more you can include in your garden native plants—whose water needs reflect the amount of local rainfall—the less irrigation you will have to do.
7. Plants need less water in cool months of the year.

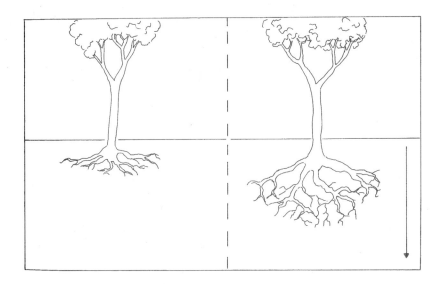

*Plants that get frequent amounts of a little bit of water never develop deep roots (left) and are vulnerable to wind damage. Heavy watering less often gets the soil wet much farther down, and roots grow deeper (right).*

In summer, plants need more water not only because the soil moisture evaporates faster in warm temperatures, but because the plant also loses water vapor through the leaves at a faster rate. This is called *transpiration*, the plant's equivalent of breathing. Wind accelerates the process, and at times the plant loses moisture through its leaves faster than it can pick it up through the roots. When that happens, the plant visibly wilts.

## When and How Much

Water when the soil is dry. I do not mean that to sound flippant. There is nothing to be gained, and much to be lost, by watering soil that does not need it. Your only answer is to become familiar with the soil in your garden, and keep a mental record.

Most vegetables and annual flowers have roots that extend down between 10 and 18 inches; most perennials, 1 to 2 feet. So for areas where these plants are planted, 18 to 24 inches is the critical depth. For simplicity of calculation and to give yourself a bit of margin, let's round up to 2 feet. What you need to determine is how long it takes for your soil to become dry 2 feet down.

Several different times a year, during one growing season, dig down that far and see whether the soil is wet. Now consider: How long has it been since it rained? With those two facts in mind, you'll begin to develop a sense of how well your soil retains water in different seasons and different rain conditions. It may come out to something like this: late spring, water after two weeks of no rain; midsummer, little or no rain, water once a week.

You need to do this digging and checking only during one growing season. Once you know your soil's basic character, you only need to make minor adjustments to account for unusual weather.

How much water does it take to wet the soil 2 feet down? Again, take the trouble to figure this out once, and you'll never have to do it again. Here's how:

Water a test area with hose or sprinkler (whatever you will be using in the garden normally) for 5 minutes. Dig down until you hit dry soil. Measure. If it's wet only 6 inches down, you know you have to water for 20 minutes to reach 2 feet.

> Early to midmorning is the ideal time to water, if circumstances give you a choice in the matter.

## Watering Techniques and Paraphernalia

If you have, or plan to install, an automatic watering system, most of the information in this section is moot. Otherwise, you have a choice of what type of watering device to use.

Oscillating sprinklers of various types are probably the most common. They deliver a broad sweep of water well, which makes them a good choice for lawns. However, as hinted at earlier, a lot of their water is lost to evaporation before it ever hits the ground. Smaller sprinklers that put out a tight, low spray are somewhat better in that respect. Better still are soaker hoses.

Soaker hoses are laid on the ground right around the plants to be watered. The hoses come in two types. One type has tiny holes all along its length, sending out extremely small, fine sprays of water wherever the hose is laid. The second type doesn't spray at all, but releases water through the pores of the material, in a

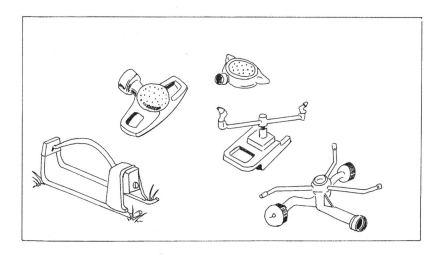

*Many types of sprinklers are available. The oscillating type (far left) makes a broad sweep, good for lawns; the others spray small and large circles, good for smaller beds.*

steady ooze. In both cases the ground is soaked—hence the name—and minimal water is lost to evaporation.

There is another advantage as well: when irrigation water doesn't get on the plant's foliage, you reduce the likelihood of mildew (see the chapter on Problems), a serious fungus disease that thrives in damp conditions.

Another way to avoid overhead watering and thus combat mildew is to dig out

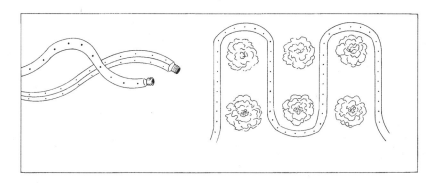

*Soaker hoses put out a steady ooze of water, soaking the ground but giving up very little to evaporation. Loop them around plants (right) for the most effective irrigation.*

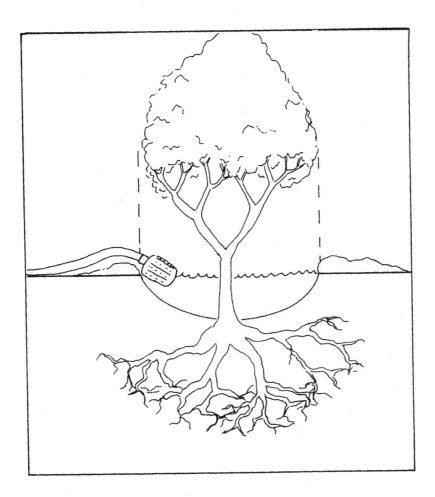

*The drip line of a tree (or small shrub, as here) is the outer edge of the area covered by the leaves. Inside the drip line, the soil stays much drier, for the leaves hold off water. Flood a basin inside the drip line to compensate.*

a small watering circle around individual plants, a sort of moat, and fill it with water directly from the hose. The walls of the moat keep the water right around the plant, instead of running off in all directions where it may not be needed.

### TREES AND SHRUBS
It is important to water new trees and shrubs during the first year after planting, and all trees and shrubs during dry periods. Here's why:

Evergreen trees and shrubs, and deciduous plants when they are leafed out, create a kind of umbrella for themselves. The leaf canopy, as it's called, does a very nice job of holding off water, as you know if you have ever taken shelter under a tree in a rainstorm.

Unfortunately, it also does a pretty good job keeping water from around the root zone. To compensate, gardeners water inside the drip line—the imaginary circle formed by the outer edges of the branches—when rainfall is scarce (see page 231).

Otherwise, regular watering is less of a problem with trees and shrubs than with smaller plants because their deeper roots do a good job of finding water.

## Conservation

Sometimes it seems that we have all the water we will ever need; just turn on the faucet and there it is. In many parts of our country, however, we are being forced to recognize that that is simply not true. As the naturally arid states attract more and more residents, the level of water usage increases exponentially, and so does our need to use this precious resource intelligently.

For starters, we must all do the initial homework to learn what is the optimal amount of water for our particular plants and our particular soil. There is no shortcut for figuring this out, but on the other hand it is not difficult. And it's important.

Then, two simple changes you can make today to save water in the garden are mulching and adding organic material to the soil.

- *Mulch*, by covering the soil, instantly and automatically reduces evaporation loss. It has another effect as well: by keeping the soil around the plant cooler in very hot weather, it slows down the transpiration rate, so plants need to take in less water from the soil. Mulch is great, too, for holding down weeds, which, among other nasty habits, rob water from the plants.
- *Organic material* dramatically improves the quality of every kind of soil, in many respects. In terms of wise water use, the benefit to sandy soil is that it holds on to water that would otherwise drain away quickly. In clay soil, it improves the texture so that too much water is not trapped.

Finally, all of us, but especially those who live in arid regions, have an obligation to think about responsible water usage as we decide how to lay out our garden and choose which plants to put in. As a new gardener, making those choices for the first time, you have a wonderful opportunity to do something good for the planet.

The easiest way to reduce the need for water is to incorporate native plants wherever you can. Plants that have evolved in an area have an innate toughness for the conditions of that area. When gardeners, chasing their own vision of what is beautiful, bring in plants from other environments, they are exacerbating what is already an artificial landscape by forcing it to grow plants with different needs. The pioneers who settled the Great Plains and insisted on growing lawns like those they had left in New England started a trend from which Americans still have not recovered.

## XERISCAPING

When the population of the West and Southwest started to explode in the second half of the twentieth century, the water supply became a serious concern. Gradually, through necessity and education, a conservation frame of mind grew, and home gardens and public landscapes began to exhibit wise-water principles. In the early 1980s, the Denver Water Board took the lead in collecting water-saving gardening ideas and developing new ones, and christened the result *xeriscaping*, derived from the Greek word for *dry*.

Xeriscaping does not mean *no* water; it means less water. It means taking water needs into account when planning gardens, and emphasizing plant and design choices with lower needs for irrigation.

Practicing xeriscaping means:

- *Good planning.* Think about water as you design your garden. Choose plants and varieties that don't need lots of water. Put moisture-loving plants together, so you can concentrate water where it is truly needed. Plant vegetable beds intensely. Put flowering annuals, with their higher water needs, up close, where you can appreciate them.
- *Good watering practices.* Use mulch, improve the water-holding capacity of the soil with organic matter, and water efficiently (use only as much as needed, and change your habits as weather conditions change).
- *Smaller lawns.* Lawn grasses consume more water than anything else in a garden. If you're putting in a new lawn, consider carefully how large a lawn area you *really* need.

**WEATHER**

*W*e all know all the cliches about the weather, but the simple fact remains: we cannot do anything to change it. All we can do is adjust our gardening practices, and find some clever ways to circumvent it.

Three aspects of weather that are important for gardens are wind, sunlight, and temperature. To varying degrees, we can manipulate the amount and intensity of each.

## Wind

Wind affects garden plants in several ways: The winter wind chill factor increases cold on your plants just as much as it does on you. So if you live in areas of high wind, during the winter you need to be extra careful about protecting against cold (see page 238).

Another concern is the drying effect of wind. Be especially alert in hot, dry weather. You will need to water more often if it is windy. Container gardens are particularly vulnerable.

And of course there is the danger of physical damage: plants blown over or limbs ripped off in high winds. If winds are a concern in your area, stake tall plants (see page 127) or tie limbs loosely together so winds can't whip them around.

Tall, dense hedges can do double-duty as windbreaks. Position them between your vulnerable plants and the prevailing wind patterns.

## Sunlight

Sunlight is essential. All plants need light for photosynthesis, the process by which they manufacture their food. We human beings can do nothing to affect the amount of sun-

*In summer (left), the sun travels a higher path through the sky. In winter, shadows are longer on any same spot and light is less intense.*

light available, and only a little to alter the amount that individual plants receive. What we *can* do is pay attention.

Let's start by remembering some basics from science class. The sun travels through the sky on different arcs at different times of the year. For gardeners, this means that one specific square foot in your garden will get different amounts of sunshine as the seasons progress. The first year, keep track of these patterns. I recommend writing your notes in your garden journal, so you can refer to them when planning next year.

Opportunities for increasing light are few. It is mostly a matter of removing obstructions. If possible, remove unwanted plants and prune away branches from nearby trees. Decreasing sunlight, on the other hand, is mostly important in vegetable gardens, and then only when you are trying to protect cool-season vegetables in hot weather. Create shade by installing roll-up blinds on a fence, using temporary screens around the plants, or deliberately planting things where they will be shaded by other plants (see page 221, for example).

So much emphasis is placed on sun requirements, we tend to think that nothing will grow in the shade. Luckily, this is not true. All plants need some sunshine, and plants that flower need a lot, but that leaves a great deal of middle ground. That middle ground is called "partial shade," and it encompasses everything between full sun and deep shade. My advice is, if in doubt, try it anyway. Many garden plants will tolerate less sun than would be considered ideal.

Also, there are many wonderful plants that do quite nicely in shade. See the lists on pages 6 (annuals), 123 (perennials), 65 (ground cover), 187, 188 (shrubs).

# Temperature

Much of the written information about garden plants has to do with temperature. The terms *tender*, *hardy*, and *half-hardy* all describe relative ability to survive cold weather. Most frequent of all are the references to zones.

### USDA HARDINESS ZONES

The U.S. Department of Agriculture produces (and periodically updates) a map of the United States that delineates eleven hardiness zones. The single piece of information that determines a zone is temperature: the lowest wintertime temperature. Zone 1, the coldest, sees winters of minus 50 degrees and below; Zone 11 never gets below 40 degrees, even in the dead of winter. (The temperature ranges represented by the eleven zones are averages; the nasty surprises of unusual weather are, by definition, impossible to predict and chart.)

It is critical to know what zone you're in simply because the information is so widely used in garden references. Almost all catalogs and many books and mag-

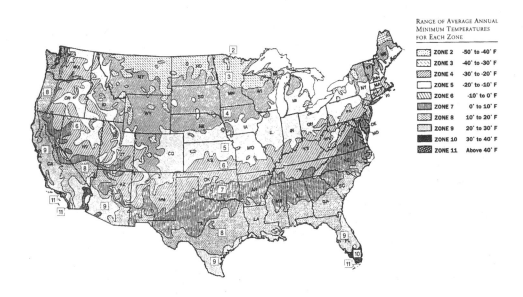

RANGE OF AVERAGE ANNUAL
MINIMUM TEMPERATURES
FOR EACH ZONE

| | ZONE 2 | -50° to -40° F |
| | ZONE 3 | -40° to -30° F |
| | ZONE 4 | -30° to -20° F |
| | ZONE 5 | -20° to -10° F |
| | ZONE 6 | -10° to 0° F |
| | ZONE 7 | 0° to 10° F |
| | ZONE 8 | 10° to 20° F |
| | ZONE 9 | 20° to 30° F |
| | ZONE 10 | 30° to 40° F |
| | ZONE 11 | Above 40° F |

*The USDA Hardiness Zone map divides the country into eleven zones, by coldest winter temperature. Most garden books and mail-order catalogs refer to these zones in their descriptions of individual plants.*

azines designate specific plants as being "hardy to Zone 6," for instance. That means that in Zone 6 and up (higher numbers equal higher temperatures), this plant should survive normal winters. In Zone 5 and colder, it would be questionable.

The focus on temperature makes sense when you think about it: no matter how careful you are in every other respect, if your plants cannot tolerate your coldest weather, they will die. But you must always remember that the zone information is one-dimensional. Whether or not you can successfully grow certain plants in your garden involves many other aspects of weather—humidity, wind, rainfall, days of sunshine—in addition to the particular microclimates in your own yard. Not to mention all the variables of good care and good luck.

To show you how weird this can be, here is an example. I live in western Oregon, which in spite of its high latitude has mild winters; it also has high rainfall, relatively few days of sunshine, and short summers. As it happens, I grew up in (and helped my grandmother garden in) South Carolina, which also has mild winters but many more days of sunshine and much longer, hotter summers. And guess what: both are in the same zone! I know for a fact that many of the flowers and vegetables I remember from my childhood cannot be grown in my current backyard, even though a seed catalog might give that impression.

The moral of the story is, learn your zone, buy plants and seeds accordingly, but don't forget there is more to gardening than temperature zones.

> *Tip:* Some mail order catalogs indicate your zone on your mailing label.

### FROST

The other aspect about cold temperatures that you need to learn is the concept of a *killing frost*. Frost—moisture condensed into ice crystals—can form whenever the temperature drops below 32 degrees and there is sufficient water vapor in the air. If the temperature is at or just below freezing, and if the plant in question is reasonably hardy, a frost is not always fatal. But in each region there comes a time when the temperatures drop to such a point that tender plants (annuals and borderline perennials) will freeze—and that is a killing frost.

The last time that point is reached in spring is referred to as the "last killing frost"; the first time it happens at the end of the summer is the "first frost." In between is your growing season. Weather statistics maintained over many years have given us enough information to establish average frost dates. Obviously unusual weather flukes will happen; you have to be satisfied with an average. Your County Extension office can help you with dates for your area.

# *Protecting Against Extremes of Weather*

### TOO HOT

1. Water the soil well, then mulch heavily. This holds moisture, with its cooling effect, in the soil.
2. Spray vulnerable plants in the heat of the afternoon if they start to wilt.
3. Add some kind of temporary shade (see suggestions on page 234). Even a leafy branch stuck in the soil can cast enough shade to protect young plants.

### TOO COLD

1. Cover individual plants with burlap or plastic, stretched over stakes (don't let leaves touch the cover-up material directly).
2. Build a perimeter fence with stakes and burlap or plastic; completely encircle a rose bed or area of perennials.
3. Mulch heavily around the bases of roses and shrubs.
4. Dig up plants and transfer them to containers that can be moved into a more sheltered location.

The best thing you can do to protect against cold weather is to not plant things that can't survive it. Choose only varieties that are hardy in your climate. And think about frost protection when you decide where to plant. Put vulnerable

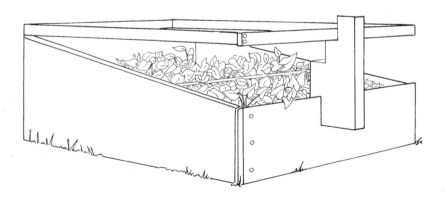

*A cold frame creates a mini-environment that is warmer than the surrounding air, allowing you to start or grow vegetables out of season. The clear top lets in sunlight, but needs to be vented.*

plants in your more sheltered spots (near the house or garage, for instance), and not at the bottom of an incline (cold air sinks).

### COLD FRAMES

All gardeners who must cope with cold weather lust for a greenhouse. If you have one, you can skip the rest of this chapter. If not, you might want to build or buy a cold frame. (See illustration on page 237.)

A cold frame is essentially a bottomless box with a clear glass or plastic top. Even when frosts descend on the garden, it is considerably warmer in the cold frame, so some provision for venting it is necessary.

People use cold frames in the spring to start new seedlings and harden off those that were started indoors. They are valuable in fall for protecting tender plants in containers, giving necessary cold treatment to potted bulbs, and even as a mini-garden for low-growing vegetables like lettuce.

# Extending the Season

Vegetable gardeners who live where summers are short must learn ways to extend the warm weather at both ends: in spring and fall, tricking Mother Nature into thinking it is warmer than it actually is. Here are some of the tricks:

1. Lay a sheet of black plastic over the soil in midspring; it will heat the soil so well that you can plant about two weeks earlier than normal. Cut Xs into the plastic and plant seeds or transplants right through the plastic.
2. Floating row covers (see page 217) also warm soil.
3. Soil in raised beds is warmer than the ground-level soil surrounding them.
4. Insert several stakes around plants and wrap clear plastic all around. Tomato cages work well for this; just place them over a plant (tomato or otherwise) and pull a plastic bag from the dry cleaners over the cage.
5. Build a collection of large translucent containers (plastic milk jugs with the bottom cut away or large glass jars) to cover small vegetable plants during the "iffy" days of early autumn. Collectively, these are called *hot caps* or *cloches*; there are also commercial versions.

## YEAR-ROUND CARE

*T*his closing chapter is something of a summary: all the principal pleasures (or chores, depending on the circumstances of the day) that gardeners engage in as the seasons unfold. You will, I am sure, recognize that the following seasonal breakdown represents only very general guidelines. For those tasks that are quite weather-dependent, you will have to enlist the aid of your gardening mentors or the smart folks at your County Extension office to learn specific dates for your area.

Because weather patterns are so varied across the country, material in this chapter is presented by season rather than month. Thus, you will prune spring-flowering shrubs in "early summer"—whenever early summer comes around in your neck of the woods.

How-to descriptions and more details on all these chores are found in the relevant chapters in this book.

## *Winter*

- Go through last year's garden journal. Make notes of what worked and what didn't, what you liked and what you're ready to replace.
- Look again at your overall garden plan. Do you want to rethink any of it?
- Spread out all the catalogs you have received. Start making comparative lists of prices and varieties of the plants you're considering.
- Periodically check mulch around shrubs and perennials. Replace if needed.
- Snow is a good mulch; don't remove it from around plants. Do, however, knock it off limbs of young trees; they could break under the weight.
- Plants under the roof overhang might need watering. Check the soil after a heavy rain; if it's drier than the rest of your garden, add water.

# Late Winter

- If you had fungal diseases on your roses last year, you might want to spray them toward the end of winter with a sulfur fungicide.
- This is a good time to take a soil sample in for testing, if you haven't already done it in prior years.
- Plant deciduous trees if the ground is not frozen.

# Early Spring

- Plant peas and onions as soon as you can work the ground (not frozen, not too soggy).
- Order seeds and plants from catalogs.
- Cut branches of flowering shrubs and bring them inside to flower.
- Check branches of shrubs and trees; prune out any damaged in winter.
- Start seeds of cool-weather vegetables indoors.
- Prune trees and shrubs that bloom in summer.
- Tune up and sharpen lawnmower and other tools.
- Plant new roses, shrubs, ground covers.
- Prune roses (in warmer areas).

# Mid to Late Spring

- Begin soil preparation to get ready for planting. Spread compost over vegetable and flower beds.
- Plant annuals in warm areas.
- Set out transplants of cool-weather vegetables. Use "collars" to control root maggots.
- Prune roses (colder climates).
- Divide perennials if needed.
- Plant summer bulbs (dahlia, gladiolus, etc.).
- Fertilize evergreen trees and flowering shrubs.
- Lawn repair, if needed: dethatch and aerate.
- Fertilize lawn in areas where cool-season grasses dominate.

- Start the weed patrol.
- If you're planning to put in a new sod lawn, this is a good time to do it.

## Early Summer

- Plant warm-season vegetables.
- Plant fall flowers such as chrysanthemums.
- Watch for cabbage moths and cucumber beetles on vegetables; use floating row covers or pick off by hand.
- Watch carefully for aphids; spray off with hose before they get a foothold.
- Deadhead flowers from spring-flowering shrubs.
- Prune spring-flowering shrubs when blossoms end.
- Plant annual flowers in colder climates.
- Order autumn-flowering bulbs.
- Stake the taller flowers while they're still a manageable height.
- Keep an eye on rainfall and water if needed.

## Mid to Late Summer

- Regularly fertilize blooming annuals and vegetables.
- Be vigilant about watering. Add lots of mulch material.
- Harvest vegetables when they're ready, whether you are ready for them or not.
- Give houseplants a vacation outside.
- Fertilize and water lawn.
- Watch for harmful insects that thrive in warm weather; spray all vulnerable plants with a hard spray from the hose once a week, just in case.
- Plant new cool-season vegetables for a fall harvest.
- If you will be putting in a new lawn this fall, begin preparing the soil in late summer.

## Early Autumn

- Dig up tender summer bulbs and prepare for winter storage.
- Carefully check houseplants for insects they may have picked up outdoors, then bring back inside.
- Plant new lawn (sod or seed); add new grass seed to bare patches on lawn.
- Plant hardy perennials.
- Plant new ground covers.
- Rake leaves and add to compost pile.

## Mid to Late Autumn

- Plant spring bulbs; also garlic.
- Plant bulbs in pots for indoor forcing.
- Plant (or move) evergreen shrubs and trees.
- Mulch around roses and flowering shrubs for winter protection.
- Remove annual flowers that have stopped blooming. Spread compost or mulch.
- Cut roses back to prevent wind damage in winter.
- Clean up all yard debris; disease pathogens may overwinter.
- Clean, oil, and store garden tools.

*Note:* If a certain gardening term is the topic of an entire chapter in this book, it is not included here.

**Acid.** Used in reference to soil: anything lower than 7.0 on the pH scale. Plants that do better in this soil are called "acid-loving."

**Aggressive.** When used in relation to plants, this means something that grows fast and spreads, and will take over its area if unchecked.

**Air layering.** A method of propagation that forces an upright stem to grow a new set of roots. Only after it is rooted is that part of the stem cut away from the plant.

**Alkaline.** In reference to soil, anything higher than 7.0 on the pH scale.

**Apical dominance.** The name for a certain growth pattern: The plant produces growth only from the tip. The apical bud (the one at the apex of the stem) suppresses all side buds. They grow only when the tip bud is removed.

**Bedding plant.** Any plant which is planted en masse in a bed. Almost always means, and sometimes is used as synonym for, annuals.

**Bolt.** Suddenly grow rapidly. Usually happens to cool-season vegetables in hot weather. The formerly small plant turns into a tall, stretched-out stem with a few (tasteless) leaves and flower head at top.

**Broadleaf.** Usually used in conjunction with "evergreen." A broadleaf evergreen has flat, more or less broad leaves, as distinct from trees or shrubs whose foliage is needle-shaped or scalelike. A rhododendron is a broadleaf evergreen.

**Cane.** The stems of certain plants, especially roses.

**Clay.** Soil that contains very small particles. The adjective is "clayey." Clay soil holds water very tightly, and so is often described as "heavy."

**Conifer.** Any plant that produces cones. Conifers can be trees or shrubs. They are almost always evergreen and have needle foliage.

**Crown.** In perennials and houseplants, the base of the plant, from which new growth emerges. In trees, the top of the tree: leaves, branches, flowers, and fruit together constitute the crown.

**Cultivar.** A variety produced in a greenhouse, rather than a natural evolution. The word itself holds its meaning: *culti*vated *vari*ety.

**Cutting.** A piece of a plant (a leaf, a section of a stem, or a root section) deliberately removed from a plant for the purpose of growing another plant. Stem cuttings, very common with houseplants, are sometimes called "slips."

**Deciduous.** The term for plants that lose all their leaves in the fall.

**Division.** A method of propagation that involves separating a plant into two or more portions by cutting through the foliage, the crown, and the roots.

**Espalier.** This word is used as a verb, for the process of fastening a tree or shrub into a rigid pattern against a wall or fence, and a noun, for the resulting form. Done for decorative purposes or, with fruit trees, to maximize fruit production in a small space.

**Evergreen.** The term for plants that have some leaves all the time. Broad-leaved evergreens (example: rhododendron) have flat, broad leaves; needle-leaved evergreens (example: pine tree) have needles instead of broad leaves. In conjunction with perennials, the term means those that have leaves year-round, to distinguish from perennials that die back to the ground in winter (see Herbaceous).

**Exotic.** Among landscape plants, "exotics" are those that have been introduced to one region from somewhere else in the world, perhaps in the past, and propagated by commercial growers. It is the opposite of "native," meaning plants that are indigenous to the area in question. Most garden plants are exotics.

**Flat.** A shallow tray or container in which a number of small plants of all the same variety are sold. In many cases they were also grown in that flat in the nursery.

**Foliage.** The all-encompassing term for leaves in all shapes. Fern fronds are foliage; so are pine needles, the strappy leaves of daffodils, and the sharp spikes of spruce.

**Genus.** A grouping of plants that share some botanical characteristics. One genus (pronounced jean-us) comprises several, or many, species. The plural is *genera*.

**Habit.** A plant's natural shape and pattern of growth is its *habit*—as in "this variety has a spreading habit."

**Hardy.** Refers to a plant's relative ability to withstand cold temperatures. Often expressed in conjunction with USDA Hardiness Zones, as in "this plant is hardy to Zone 5" or "not hardy in our area." *Half-hardy* and *semihardy* are used, less precisely, to refer to plants that are normally hardy in a certain zone but not if it is unusually cold in any given year. In Europe, perennials are collectively known as "hardy plants."

**Heavy.** In reference to soil, this means a very high percentage of clay.

**Herbaceous.** A plant with a soft stem, one you could push your fingernail into, is said to be herbaceous. Mostly used in conjunction with perennials; all the aboveground parts of a herbaceous perennial die in the winter, but the roots remain alive and new aboveground growth appears the following spring.

**Hill.** A group of seeds planted close together constitutes a hill. It has nothing to do with elevation.

**Humus.** Vegetative organic matter at a specific stage of decomposition—the final stage. It is dark colored, rich looking, and extremely valuable as an ingredient in garden soil. Effectively the same as compost.

**Hybrid.** A new plant produced by crossing two different species, introducing the pollen of one into the ovary of another. Done purposefully in a laboratory to emphasize positive attributes of both parents.

**Inorganic.** Produced from synthetic materials.

**Insecticidal soap.** A type of insect control. Special fatty acids in solution are sprayed on the plant. Insects that come in contact are paralyzed. Homemade version uses liquid soap.

**Invasive.** The term for a plant that spreads and multiplies on its own, usually by underground runners. In other words, a pest.

**Leggy.** A term that describes a certain unattractive growth pattern: long stretches of bare stem, with just a few leaves or flowers. Usually caused by insufficient light, and therefore most commonly a problem with houseplants.

**Node.** The point on a stem where growing energy is concentrated. Leaves and new branches originate from nodes, and stem cuttings form roots at nodes.

**Oil.** Oil sprays are used to control insects; sprayed over the stems and leaves, they block off the oxygen for both the insects and their eggs. There are two commercial types: dormant oils, used in winter on fruit trees and certain shrubs; and summer oils, lighter and less toxic than the winter type. Homemade versions use vegetable oil.

**Organic.** Something that is, or once was, alive, either animal or vegetable, or something made from organic materials. In the garden, often signifies products of lower toxicity, but not always.

**Ornamental.** The collective term for all garden plants, to distinguish them from food crops and commercial agricultural plantings such as tree farms and market gardens.

**Peat moss.** A natural product used as a soil amendment in the garden or in containers. It is sphagnum moss crushed into a fine powder. It is very difficult to get wet, but once wet holds water for a long time.

**Perlite.** A soil amendment used principally to increase air circulation in soils that would otherwise compact too tightly together. It is made from volcanic rock that is heated to very high temperatures and then crushed into small bits. It is bright white and extremely lightweight.

**Potbound.** The term for a container plant whose roots have become so overgrown they completely fill the container, or nearly so. *Rootbound* means the same thing.

**Rootbound.** See potbound.

**Self-sow.** When a plant that produces seeds drops those seeds to the ground, and they germinate the following year. Also referred to as *seeding down.*

**Silt.** A specific type of soil, containing particles that are smaller than sand but larger than clay.

**Species.** In the world of gardening this word has two meanings, somewhat related. A species is the smallest group in the basic classification system developed in the eighteenth century (also see Genus). In modern times many subspecies, varieties, and cultivars have been added. The second meaning is as the "wild" variety of any plant, the one that would be found in nature, unmanipulated by the horticulture industry. Thus we speak of "species rhododendrons" or "species tulips"—the parents of all commercial hybrid rhodies or tulips.

**Sphagnum moss.** An organic soil amendment used in the garden or in containers. It is actual moss, collected and dried. It resembles a snarl of gray-green knitting yarn. Peat moss is made from it.

**Sucker.** A new stem that emerges from the root area, in competition with the main stem. Should be removed.

**Systemic.** Something that affects a plant's entire *system.* Usually used in reference to a group of all-purpose fungicides and insecticides.

**Tender.** The opposite of hardy.

**Tilth.** The texture of soil.

**Tip layering.** A propagation method in which a long stem of a plant is buried while it still attached to the plant, and cut away as a new plant when roots have formed. Also see air layering.

**Variegated.** More than one color; usually used in reference to leaves. Variegated foliage may show two colors (usually green plus one other), be tricolor, or multicolor. The additional color may be stripes, swirls, polka dots, or borders.

**Variety.** A subunit of a species. Either the result of natural evolution or, more likely, greenhouse production.

**Vermiculite.** A soil amendment used to keep otherwise heavy soil from compacting. It is made from mica, a natural mineral formation, subjected to high heat which breaks it into small, flat plates.

**Watersprout.** A branch or stem that grows rapidly and strongly, and thus diverts nutrients from other stems. Watersprouts will distort the shape of a tree and will slow fruit production on fruit trees; they should be pruned off.

**Weeping.** A type of growth habit in which branches grow out horizontally and then turn down.

**Woody.** Hard, tough. Used in reference to stems of certain plants; the opposite of herbaceous.

**Zone.** A geographical area, defined by winter climate. The entire United States is divided into eleven zones, established by the Department of Agriculture. Horticultural reference works and catalogs often refer to zones.

## Books in a Series

The first four listed here all do a fine job of presenting general information; they are particularly appropriate for new gardeners. Each series comprises many titles on specific topics, such as Lawns, Roses, Vegetables, and so on.

"American Gardening" series from Burpee. A good all-around introduction to many specific topics.

"Expert" series. All written by D. G. Hessayon, and all excellent.

The "All About . . ." series from Ortho Books. Good overviews of the specific topic. *All About Roses* is particularly recommended.

Sunset Books. How-to books on a wealth of garden topics, all with first-rate information.

Random House gardening series: *Random House Book of . . .* [Trees, Perennials, Roses, etc.] These books may seem a bit overwhelming to beginners, but take a look at them anyway. When you're ready for comprehensive guides to plant identification, these are outstanding.

## Individual Books

*The American Horticultural Society Encyclopedia of Gardening.* Christopher Brickell, ed. New York: Dorling Kindersley, 1994. Big, heavy, authoritative.

American Rose Society. *Handbook for Selecting Roses.* Published each year. PO Box 30,000, Shreveport, LA 71130. $5.

Ashmun, Barbara. *The Garden Design Primer.* New York: Lyons & Burford, 1993. Presents the abstract concepts of design in an understandable way, and makes them tangible with lots of plant suggestions. Light on photos, but heavy on ideas.

Barton, Barbara. *Gardening by Mail*. Boston: Houghton Mifflin, 1994 (rev. ed.). A directory of all kinds of mail-order resources, plus access information on plant societies, libraries, and recommended books, magazines, and newsletters, some of them hard to find.

Brickell, Christopher. *Pruning*. New York: Fireside, 1988. Awesomely detailed but very followable. Everything you will ever need to know about pruning is illustrated here.

Damrosch, Barbara. *The Garden Primer*. New York: Workman Publishing, 1988. Covers all the basics with good information and a pleasant style.

Ferguson, Nicola. *Right Plant, Right Place*. New York: Summit Books, 1984. Essentially a book of lists: plant suggestions for every possible gardening condition.

Harper, Pamela. *Designing with Perennials*. New York: Macmillan, 1991. All of Ms. Harper's works are worth dipping into.

Johnson, Hugh. *Principles of Gardening*. New York: Fireside, 1979. Excellent all-purpose gardening reference, also good for plant identification.

Reader's Digest. *Illustrated Guide to Gardening*. 1995. Very comprehensive.

Rodale. *Encyclopedia of Organic Gardening*. Emmaus, PA: Rodale Press, 1992. Very comprehensive information (almost 700 pages long), with Rodale's well-known organic approach.

Royal Horticultural Society. *Colour Dictionary of Garden Plants*. 1969. Excellent for plant identification. Focus is on British plants, most of which grow in NE and NW United States.

Seymour, E.L.D., ed. *Garden Encyclopedia*. New York: Wise & Co., 1936. This classic book (fondly known as "Wise's Encyclopedia") is out of print but a treasure. If you ever see a copy, grab it. No color photos, but very comprehensive information on thousands of plants. As older varieties come back into vogue, books like this become especially valuable.

Sunset Books. *Western Garden Book.* Menlo Park, CA: Sunset Publishing, 1995 rev. ed. If you live in Arizona, California, Colorado, Idaho, Montana, Nevada, New Mexico, Oregon, Utah, Washington, or Wyoming, this is your bible. Even if you don't, it's a valuable resource. I cannot imagine gardening without it.

# Magazines

Through the many color photos in these magazines, you can visit some of the best-designed gardens in the country. Good ideas are not patented; you can borrow them any time you want.

I recommend browsing through several back issues of all of these, to see which you especially like. Subscription addresses are included here.

Country Living Gardener
PO Box 7335, Red Oak, IA 51591-0335; 800-777-0102

Fine Gardening
Taunton Press, PO Box 5506, Newton, CT 06470-5506

Flower & Gardening
PO Box 7507, Red Oak, IA 51591-0507

Garden Gate
2200 Grand Ave., Des Moines, IA 50312; 800-978-9631

Horticulture
PO Box 53879, Boulder, CO 80321

National Gardening
PO Box 52874, Boulder, CO 80322-2874; 800-727-9097

Organic Gardening
33 E. Minor St., Emmaus, PA 18098; 610-967-5171

The companies that appear here are some of my personal favorites; I especially admire them for the attention they devote to including information about growing their products. But this list is not, by any stretch of the imagination, comprehensive. Many fine places sell plants or seeds by mail order. To find others, check Barbara Barton's *Gardening by Mail* (see Bookshelf), note their ads in gardening magazines, or write to the Mail Order Gardening Association for the current *Garden Catalog Guide,* their directory of member organizations. (PO Box 2129, Columbia, MD 21045; $2.)

Bluestone Perennials
7211 Middle Ridge Road
Madison, OH 44057
Ph: 800-852-5243
      Hardy perennials

W. Atlee Burpee Gardens
300 Park Ave.
Warminster, PA 18974
Ph: 800-888-1447
Fax: 800-487-5530
      Seeds and plants

The Cook's Garden
PO Box 535
Londonderry, VT 05148
Ph: 802-824-3400
Fax: 802-824-3027
      Vegetables

Edmunds Roses
6235 SW Kahle Rd.
Wilsonville, OR 97070
Ph: 503-682-1476
Fax: 503-682-1275
      Roses

Harris Seeds
PO Box 22960
Rochester, NY 14692
Ph: 800-514-4441
Fax: 716-442-9386
      Vegetable and flower seeds

Heirloom Old Garden
      Roses
24062 NE Riverside Dr.
St Paul, OR 97137
Ph: 503-538-1576
Fax: 503-538-5902
      Old roses

Jackson & Perkins
PO Box 1028
Medford, OR 97501
Ph: 800-292-4769
Fax: 800-242-0329
      Roses, perennials

Johnny's Selected Seeds
230 Foss Hill Rd.
Albion, ME 04910-9731
Ph: 207-437-4301
Fax: 800-437-4290
　　Seeds for flowers, vegetables, herbs

Klehm Nursery
4210 North Duncan Rd.
Champion, IL 61821
Ph: 800-553-3715
Fax: 217-373-8403
E-mail: klehm@soltec.net
Web site: http://www.klehm.com
　　Perennials

Nichols Garden Nursery
1190 North Pacific Highway
Albany, OR 97321
Ph: 541-928-9280
Fax: 541-967-8406
　　Vegetable and flower seeds

Park Seed Co.
PO Box 46
Cokesbury Rd.
Greenwood, SC 29648-0046
Ph: 800-845-3369
Fax: 800-275-9941; 864-941-4206
　　Flower and vegetable seeds

Pinetree Garden Seed
PO Box 300
New Gloucester, ME 04260
Ph: 207-926-3400
Fax: 888-527-3337
　　Seeds for vegetables, flowers, herbs

Prairie Nursery
PO Box 306
Westfield, WI 53964
Ph: 608-296-3679
Fax: 608-296-2741
　　Wildflowers, native grasses

Shepherd's Garden Seeds
30 Irene St.
Torrington, CT 06790
Ph: 860-482-3638
Fax: 860-482-0532
　　Vegetables, flowers, herbs

Thompson & Morgan
PO Box 1308
Jackson, NJ 08527
Ph: 800-274-7333
Fax: 908-363-9356
　　Everything under the sun

White Flower Farms
PO Box 50
Litchfield, CT 06759-0050
Ph: 860-496-9600; 800-503-9624
Fax: 860-496-1418
　　Perennials, shrubs, bulbs

*G*ardening from the *ground up* explains completely, but simply, the whys behind the what-to-dos in growing a beautiful garden. This practical guide covers all the basics—preparing the ground, choosing the best varieties for your soil's needs, and tending your tender plants—with lots of illustrations to make understanding the process a snap! Dig in and learn about:

* Herbs—grow, harvest, and preserve all the basic herbs...and design your own herb garden
* Organic gardening—control diseases, insects, and other garden pests without harming the environment
* Basic botany—unearth the mysteries of pollination, bud dominance, dormancy, and other previously confusing miracles of Mother Nature
* Houseplants, container gardens, ground covers, perennials, vegetables, shrubs, and trees

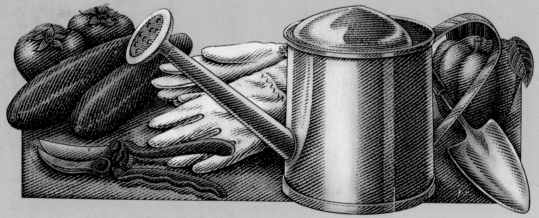

MAGGIE STUCKEY is a veteran gardener and expert on horticulture who has written many wonderful, helpful books. She can be found in her garden on any sunny day in Portland, Oregon.

Cover design by Anne Twomey
Cover illustration by Peter Siu

ST. MARTIN'S GRIFFIN
175 Fifth Avenue, New York, N.Y. 10010
Distributed by McClelland & Stewart Inc. in Canada
PRINTED IN THE U.S.A.

ISBN 0-312-18101-9

51695>

9 780312 181017